MEET JOHN PAUL II

ALSO BY JANEL RODRIGUEZ

*Meet Fulton Sheen: Beloved Preacher and Teacher of the Word*

# JOHN PAUL II

*The People's Pope*

JANEL RODRIGUEZ

SERVANT
BOOKS

PUBLISHED BY ST. ANTHONY MESSENGER PRESS
CINCINNATI, OHIO

Excerpts from *Witness to Hope: The Biography of Pope John Paul II*, by George Weigel, copyright ©1999, reprinted with permission of HarperCollins Publishers. Excerpts from The Gospel of Life *(Evangelium Vitae)*, by Pope John Paul II, ©1995, used by permission of Libreria Editrice Vaticana. Excerpts from *Pope John Paul II: The Life of My Friend Karol Wojtyla*, by Mieczyslaw Malinski, copyright ©1979, used by permission of Continuum International Publishing Group.

Scripture passages have been taken from the *Revised Standard Version*, Catholic edition. Copyright 1946, 1952, 1971 by the Division of Christian Education of the National Council of Churches of Christ in the USA. Used by permission. All rights reserved.

Cover and book design by Mark Sullivan
Cover image by © Bernard Bisson/CORBIS SYGMA

LIBRARY OF CONGRESS CATALOGING-IN-PUBLICATION DATA
Rodriguez, Janel.
Meet John Paul II : the people's Pope / Janel Rodriguez.
p. cm.
Includes bibliographical references and index.
ISBN 978-0-86716-830-3 (pbk. : alk. paper)  1. John Paul II, Pope, 1920-2005. 2. Popes—Biography. I. Title.
BX1378.5.R625 2008
282.092—dc22
[B]
2008008874

ISBN: 978-0-86716-830-3

Published by Servant Books, an imprint of St. Anthony Messenger Press.
28 W. Liberty St.
Cincinnati, OH 45202
www.ServantBooks.org

Printed in the United States of America.

Printed on acid-free paper.

08 09 10 11 12 5 4 3 2 1

For my parents, Deacon Arnaldo Rodriguez and Gladys Rodriguez, who raised me in the "domestic church" with love.

And for my "Narnians," Emily Francis Baldwin, Julia Elizabeth Flatto, Claudia Vitus Marino Dodge and Aaron Edgar Bronfman— hope of the future and dear to my heart.

# Contents

. . . . .

# *Acknowledgments*

I WISH TO THANK THOSE PEOPLE WHO GAVE ME OR LENT ME their books, videos and other media to help stock my research library while working on this book: Lois Harrigan, Arlene Orent, Wilfrid Pleau, T.O.C. and Theresa Monaco, T.O.C.

I am also grateful to those who shared their stories of encounters with the pope, helping give this book a personal touch, especially Father Marek Sotek and Mr. Carlos Padula.

My gratitude also goes out to my parents, to whom this book is dedicated, and Father Paul Denault, O. CARM., Father Jack Canning, O. CARM., Ms. Alejandra Soler-Roig and all those who supported me with their prayers.

I am also grateful to Father Kazimierz A. Kowalski, Father William Elder, Father Richard Terga, C.I.C.M. and Father Andrzej Klimek, of Our Lady of Good Counsel Church in Manhattan, for their kind understanding, encouragement and spiritual support and for together leaving me one of the best cell phone messages I have ever received.

To the Sisters of the Visitation, especially Mother Susan Marie and Sister Judith Marguerite, who allowed me the use of their beautiful monastery in Bay Ridge, Brooklyn, while I was writing this book.

I wish to thank my editors, Cindy Cavnar (who was always available to help), Lucy Scholand (who had the patience of a saint) and my sister, Jennifer Rodriguez (who was most generous with her time and talent) for all their professional editorial help. Without their understanding and *outstanding* support, this book truly would not have been written.

And to the Blessed Mother, the Black Madonna, Our Lady of Czestochowa and Mother of Mount Carmel. *Totus Tuus!*

# *Santo Subito!*

CARDINAL JOSEPH RATZINGER, HIS WHITE HAIR FLUTTERING delicately in the wind, folded his hands in prayer and looked out onto the sea of people. It was April 8, 2005, and thousands had gathered at the Vatican to take part in one of the first major historic events of the twenty-first century: the burial of one of the greatest popes to ever lead the Catholic Church, John Paul II.

As the cardinals assembled on the altar for the final blessing, the crowd broke into applause. The clapping then took on a beat: *clap-clap, clap-clap-clap; clap-clap, clap-clap-clap.* Next came shouts of *"Santo subito!"* Soon the shouts became a chant that reverberated with the clapping: *"Santo!"* (*clap-clap-clap*), *"Santo!"* (*clap-clap-clap*), *"Subito!"* (*clap-clap-clap*). "Saint! Saint! Make him a saint now! Saint! Saint! Make him a saint now!"

Cardinal Ratzinger, the main celebrant of the funeral Mass, looked on in amazement. As in the days of old, popular opinion was demanding that a holy person be officially recognized as a saint. Eleven days later Ratzinger was elected Pope Benedict XVI, and one of his first acts as pope was in response to the will of the people: He waived the standard waiting period of five years and immediately opened the cause for Pope John Paul II's canonization.

## A MIRACLE

Fast-forward to a press conference in Aix-en-Provence, France, on March 30, 2007. Lights flash from every corner of the room as photographers jostle one another to get a shot of the woman whom newspapers have dubbed "the miracle nun," but no light beams brighter than the smile of Sister Marie Simon-Pierre of the Little Sisters of Catholic Maternities. The very picture of poise, she stands in intriguing contrast to the headline-hungry press as she proclaims that she has been miraculously healed of an incurable disease, thanks to the saintly intercession of the late Pope John Paul II.

The forty-six-year-old French nun said, "I was no longer the same inside....It is difficult for me to explain....It was too strong, too big. A mystery."

After being diagnosed with Parkinson's disease in 2001, Sister Marie Simon-Pierre could not help but feel a deep kinship with the pope, who at the time was suffering from the same disease. As his health deteriorated before the world, hers did the same behind the cloister walls, her condition gradually worsening to the point where even walking was difficult. In time she lost control of both her arms: Her left arm dangled uselessly at her side, and her right hand trembled with such force that it was a struggle for her to write—and she could barely read her own scrawl. Driving, too, became impossible.

With sadness the mother superior relieved Sister Marie Simon-Pierre of the various duties that she could no longer perform properly. And whenever the community of nuns saw the ailing John Paul II on television, they were all painfully aware that their sister in community would soon be facing the same challenges. Sister Marie Simon-Pierre admitted, "I saw myself in years to come." Yet this thought strengthened the bond that she felt she had with John Paul II. "He was, in a way, my Pope," she said. She came to regard the Holy Father as both a friend and a support.

When John Paul II died on April 2, 2005, Sister Marie Simon-Pierre suffered the loss deeply. Meanwhile, her health continued its steady decline. Her community began to include in their prayers a regular plea to John Paul II. They asked that he add his prayers to theirs on Sister Marie's behalf, and that he ask the Lord to heal her.

Then it happened. One night, some two months after the sisters began asking for the pope's intercession, Sister Marie heard a voice as she entered deeply into prayer. "Write," it commanded her. She scrambled for a pen and found to her joy that she was able to write legibly and without shaking. By the next morning, feeling "completely transformed," Sister Marie Simon-Pierre presented herself to a fellow nun and thrust out her right hand. "Look," she said, "my hand is no longer shaking. John Paul II has cured me."[1]

## WHAT IS A SAINT?

The Catholic Church does not make saints; God does. The Church, however, may recognize them in a special and public way by canonizing them: pronouncing them holy to the world. The road to this official recognition may be long and arduous, as the life of the person under consideration must be thoroughly investigated and proven to meet specific criteria.

The first stage is opening a person's cause for sainthood to investigation, when he or she is given the title "Servant of God."

The second stage comes after documentation of the person's life is presented to the Congregation for the Causes of Saints in Rome. If it receives favorable judgment there, as well as the approval of the pope, the candidate is declared "Venerable" and is recognized as having lived a life of heroic virtue—one that goes markedly beyond a typically good Christian life.

The third stage follows the attribution of a miracle to that person's intercession. The miracle must be carefully investigated and accepted by the Church. The pope then beatifies the candidate, who is then titled "Blessed." This is considered the most difficult stage to reach.

It is interesting to note that a miracle is not needed in the case of a martyr, a person who was killed for testifying to the faith. It is, however, required in the cases of holy people whom the Church calls "confessors," or those, like Pope John Paul II, who lived a holy life and then closed it by a holy death in Christian peace. This "peace," some have pointed out, can involve slow and painful suffering (such as through illness), so it becomes a martyrdom of a different sort.

Lastly, sainthood is declared when a second miracle is

attributed to the intercession of the "Blessed" person and it has been investigated and approved.

Sister Marie Simon-Pierre's story of her miraculous healing gave credence to the possibility of a quick beatification and even canonization of the beloved pope. Three days after the announcement of her healing, the Church closed the official investigation into the pope's life, the second stage of the canonization process. This happened to be the second anniversary of the pope's death, and marking that anniversary Pope Benedict XVI said:

> His whole life, particularly with the slow but implacable advance of the disease which gradually stripped him of everything, became an offering to Christ, a living proclamation of his passion in hope brimming with faith in the resurrection.
>
> ...[W]e can apply to him the words of the first Song of the Servant of the Lord which we heard in the First Reading: "Behold my servant, whom I uphold, my chosen, in whom my soul delights; I have put my Spirit upon him, he will bring forth justice to the nations" (*Is* 42:1).
>
> "Servant of God": this is what he was and this is what we in the Church call him now, while the process of his Beatification continues.[2]

Will John Paul II become a canonized saint of the Church? That is "for the Church to say," Sister Marie Simon-Pierre told the press. Yet there is little question that we can profit from looking at the life and work of this holy man. Let us together meet John Paul II.

## ❦ 1 ❧

## The Good Son

IT WAS THE MORNING OF SEPTEMBER 1, 1939, AND THE SKY above Poland's Wawel Cathedral buzzed menacingly with the sound of approaching Nazi aircraft. Although it was First Friday, a day for the adoration of the Eucharist in the Roman Catholic Church, Father Kazimierz Figlewicz found himself all alone on the compound. His fellow priests, clerics and staff left in fear. As the sun rose that morning, a surprise Nazi air strike released bombs all over Poland in an explosive wake-up call.

Father Figlewicz couldn't blame the church staff for flee-ing in anticipation of the next air raid. But as he made his way to the church, he wondered how he was going to celebrate Mass without another person present. When he stepped inside the sanctuary, however, he saw that he would not be alone. Waiting for him was nineteen-year-old university student Karol Wojtyla.

As the Mass proceeded, fresh attacks began, and pandemonium erupted all around the two men. Explosions thundered and sirens wailed in a terrible herald that World War II had officially begun. Still the Mass continued. When the sacrifice was completed, Karol excused himself, telling the priest, "I've got to go, my father's at home alone."[1]

After checking on his father and finding him unharmed, Karol then stopped by the home of his friends the Kydryńskis. Finding that they too were safe, he helped them move some of their possessions to what they hoped would be a more secure location. Suddenly they were again under attack.

Although the entire house shuddered with each explosion, Karol stopped what he was doing and calmly leaned against a wall as if to support its foundation. Juliusz Kydryński marveled at his friend's serenity.[2] He did not know that he was looking at the perfect portrait of the man who would become John Paul II, a pope who was concerned for his father and his "Father's house," who was a servant of his fellow man, who was a champion of the suffering and who was an unshakable pillar of strength even when the surrounding world floundered in confusion and chaos.

## THE DOMESTIC CHURCH

Poland was a country that had suffered oppression for centuries and would continue to suffer after World War II, when the Communists would take over. But the early days of Karol's life in Poland were simple and peaceful.

Although descended from tailors and farmers, his father, Karol Wojtyla, Sr., was forced to embrace a different vocation when he was drafted into the army. He developed his military career and became an officer in the 56th Infantry Regiment of the Austro-Hungarian Army. He married Emilia Kaczorowska in 1904, and the couple moved to Wadowice in Galicia, where Karol was stationed. He eventually worked his way up to the position of first lieutenant in the 12th Infantry Regiment there.

A busy industrial town that had long housed Poland's troops, Wadowice also boasted a healthy and active cultural life. Poets, scholars and talented theater people lived side by side with the town's tradesmen, lawyers and businessmen.

Roman Catholicism was part of Poland's identity as a nation, and being devout was the norm. In Wadowice, the farmer, the philosopher, the peasant and the artist were all serious about their faith. This attitude of understanding and respect created unity among the rich and the poor, the educated and the uneducated. And this attitude extended beyond the Catholic community to a large Jewish population.

In this favorable environment Karol and Emilia Wojtyla began building a family. Their first son, Edmund, was born in 1906. Nicknamed "Mundek," he possessed a number of the same gifts his younger brother would display: athleticism, intelligence, sensitivity toward the suffering of others and an attitude of selfless giving.

Their second child, a daughter named Olga, died while still an infant. There are no official records of the exact dates of her birth and death, but her loss was undoubtedly a painful event for the family.

The third and last child was named after his father. Karol Józef Wojtyla was born on May 18, 1920. Legend has it that his mother asked the midwife to throw open the windows of the room so that the first sound the baby heard would be that of the choir of St. Mary's Church, which was directly across the square.[3] Whether this is true or not, the Wojtylas certainly were a religious family. Karol was baptized in the Roman Catholic Church at St. Mary's on June 20, 1920.[4]

Emilia's pride was typical of a loving mother. As she proudly pushed the baby carriage down the street, she would tell people that Karol would grow up to be "a great man some day."[5] She was not the first mother to say such things about her child. But her prophecy would prove true.

The Wojtylas' life was a simple one. Karol, Sr., regularly reported for duty at his station in town, Emilia contributed what she could to the family earnings by taking in sewing, teenaged Edmund studied medicine at Jagiellonian University and little Karol— nicknamed "Lolek"—would play with his friends, such as Regina "Ginka" Beer, the daughter of the Wojytlas' neighbors.

Karol began attending Marcin Wadowita School when he was six years old. The small school occupied the top two floors of the Wadowice district court building, a stone's throw from the Wojtyla home. His grades were always good, and in some subjects, such as religion and singing, they were "very good."[6]

Karol's athleticism showed itself early. He loved to play soccer with his friends, including his schoolmate Boguslaw Banas, whose parents ran the neighborhood dairy and café. The boys kicked and scrambled in the apartment courtyard under the protective gaze of Emilia and other mothers, who sat together nearby.[7] Lolek was often goalie, a defensive position that, depending on whom you asked, he played well or not so well.

Soccer was not the boys' only pastime. Boguslaw remembers an occasional game of "Mass," a typical interest for young Polish Catholics of the time. While Boguslaw and his brother attended as servers, Lolek would preside over an altar table upon which stood "a holy picture and two candles." He wore "a worsted cape," made by his mother's loving hands, "over…a kind of alb."[8]

## A SAD PARTING

Emilia's health had always been delicate. In 1927 she was ill enough that her husband decided to retire from the army to care for her. Reduced to living on his small pension, meeting expenses became a struggle for the Wojtylas.

On April 13, 1929, Karol was called home from school and given sad news. Emilia had died at the age of forty-five. The official cause of death was heart and kidney failure. Lolek was not yet nine years old.

Edmund, who had been at university for a year, came home for the funeral, then quickly went back to school to resume his studies. Lolek, on the other hand, made a pilgrimage with his father to the nearby town of Kalwaria Zebrzydowska, in Kraków, and stopped at its shrine dedicated to the Virgin Mary. There Lolek knelt before her image, in which she held the baby Jesus, and prayed that her Son would have mercy on the soul of his late mother.

Lolek received his First Communion a month later. That day he also received a scapular from the Carmelite friars in Wadowice, and this he wore for the rest of his life. He would later feel a special connection to that religious order and even try to join it before discovering that God had other plans for him.

Young Lolek and his father slowly and stoically adjusted to their new life together. Their tragic loss drew them closer together, both emotionally and literally. They moved their beds into the same room and avoided the parlor, which they identified with Emilia. Lolek's father soon took over the cooking duties, making breakfast and dinner on a daily basis. Lunch was shared at the Banas family's café.[9]

Day by day the relationship between father and son deepened, as did Lolek's admiration for his father, whom he considered "a deeply religious man." Lolek saw his mother's death intensify the spiritual life of his father to such a degree that he became a man "of constant prayer." Lolek would awaken in the middle of the night and discern in the dark the figure of his father kneeling in prayer. His father's example, Pope John Paul II would realize upon reflection later, was his "*first seminary.*"[10]

There were also moments of great fun. The elder Karol encouraged his son's love of soccer, even allowing him to kick a ball around the parlor. With its rolled-up rugs and shrouded furniture, the room they had all but abandoned after Emilia's death became an ideal indoor playing field on rainy days. Even the lieutenant joined the game, vigorously trying to kick the ball past Lolek, who played goalie as usual.[11]

## FAITHFUL FRIENDS

The attitude of understanding and respect among "Wawros" (as people from Wadowice were called) extended to the Jewish population. Numbering around two thousand, the Jews made up about a quarter of the population. The Wojtylas were friends with a number of Jewish families, and they rented their apartment, at what was then Number 2 Rynek Street, from the Balamuths, a Jewish family who lived on the ground floor. Their neighbors, the Beer family, were also Jewish.

At school the Christians and Jews sometimes separated into different soccer teams, but if the Jewish team needed another player, Karol did not hesitate to join them. No one questioned him or protested when he did this. The Jewish players were, after all, schoolmates and even personal friends of Karol. They included Jerzy Kluger (called "Jurek") and Poldek Goldberger, a fellow goalkeeper.

Sadly, those carefree days of peace would disappear under the shadow of the Nazi regime. Long before the German invasion, anti-Semitism in Poland grew to the extent that the Beer family decided to go to Palestine. Karol and his father hated to see their neighbors go. When Ginka said good-bye to them, she assured the unhappy Wojtylas that their move was for the best. Young Karol she found to be beyond consolation, however. Red-faced with emotion, the young boy could neither speak nor shake her hand in parting.[12]

Karol would continue to spend time with his friend Boguslaw Banas. One afternoon, when the two were teenagers, they were hanging around the Banas family's café with Boguslaw's brother. Boguslaw opened the till and inside found a revolver. He knew to whom it belonged: a neighborhood policeman would come to the bar and have a few drinks after he completed his shift. On occasion, when he felt he had had too much to drink, he would leave the gun in the care of Boguslaw's parents.

Boguslaw had seen the gun time and again and had never been tempted to touch it. But he took the gun out of the drawer this time and for some reason aimed it directly at Karol. "Hands up, or I'll shoot," he threatened playfully.

Karol was seated on a bench five or six yards away, next to Boguslaw's brother. Before any of them knew what was happening, the gun went off. The bullet, Boguslaw remembered, missed Karol by a "hair's breadth" and pierced a nearby window. The sound of breaking glass jolted Mr. Banas from his midday nap, and he ran into the room to find three terrified teenagers. Without a word he removed the gun from his son's hand and put it away. Neither Mr. Banas nor Karol ever mentioned the incident again. Boguslaw, on the other hand, would be haunted by its memory for the rest of his life. "My God," he would think, "I might have killed the Pope."[13]

## ANOTHER MOTHER

A happy event in young Lolek's life was his big brother Edmund's graduation from college. After the ceremony the lieutenant took Lolek on his first trip to a sanctuary in the far-off hills, where they could once again give thanks to God and pray together before an image of the Blessed Mother and the child Jesus. This time it was Poland's most beloved icon of the Virgin Mary.

Nestled in the lime hills that run from Kraków to Wielun

is the city of Czestochowa [Ches-ta-ko´-va], and within that city rises the National Shrine of Poland, Jasna Góra ("Luminous Hill"). This sanctuary, run by Pauline monks, is a destination for pilgrims from all over the world. Its main attraction is the famous icon of the Black Madonna or Our Lady of Czestochowa, a distinctive portrait of a dark-skinned Blessed Mother holding an equally dark baby Jesus.

Historians believe that the skin tones could derive from any of a number of sources—exposure to incense smoke over hundreds of years being one of them—but some legends claim that Saint Luke the evangelist rendered the Blessed Mother from life, painting the image on the top of a table built by Jesus and used in the home of the Holy Family. It is believed that when he did this he accurately rendered the skin tone of the Middle Eastern woman sitting before him. Legend goes on to say that the Virgin gave the image her blessing.

If she did so, it was a powerful blessing. When an army of Hussites raided the monastery in 1430, they attacked the icon, ripping off the jewels that adorned it and slashing the Virgin's face with a sword. Then they knocked the painting down and trampled it underfoot, finally leaving it behind to spoil in the sludge and mud. But it was not destroyed. In fact, the monks recovered, washed and restored it. As they could not erase the marks left by the sword, they instead high-lighted them so that the faithful could see more vividly how the image had been both desecrated and rescued.

And this is how it appeared when miraculous events took place over the centuries that followed. Perhaps the most famous story about the powerful protection of the Black

Madonna happened in 1655. When Swedish troops moved in to attack the city, a group of faithful Polish soldiers gathered together to pray before the icon, asking for the intercession of the Blessed Mother to save Poland. Miraculously the siege halted, and the enemy retreated. One year later, on April 1, Poland's King John Casimir consecrated his country to the Blessed Mother, declaring her the Queen of Poland and Czestochowa the spiritual capital of the country.

Another miracle, perhaps even greater than that one, occurred just a few months after Lolek was born in 1920. The Soviet Russian Army, planning an invasion of Warsaw, menacingly assembled on the bank of the Vistula River. Once again the Polish people—this time soldiers and citizens alike—appealed fervently to Our Lady of Czestochowa. They received a sign on the Feast of Our Lady of Sorrows, when a vision of Our Lady materialized in the sky above Warsaw. This provided the people with consolation, and although the Russians still attacked, the Poles fought them back in a series of battles that led to their ultimate victory, which was later called "The Miracle at the Vistula."

Karol's visit to Jasna Góra would have a profound effect on him. Motherless at a young and impressionable age, he would only grow in his respect and veneration of the Blessed Mother over the years, eventually proclaiming that all he did for the glory of God he did through Mary, as her totally devoted servant. He would receive the sacrament of confirmation on May 3, 1938—the feast day of the Black Madonna—and a special connection and dedication to the Virgin Mary would be a hallmark of his papacy.

## BROTHER AND HERO

When Karol's brother, assistant resident Dr. Edmund Wojtyla, was assigned to the municipal hospital in nearby Bielsko, the brothers were able to see a lot more of each other. During Lolek's twelfth and thirteenth years, they finally forged the brotherly bond that they had been unable to form before because of the difference in their ages.

Mundek treated Lolek to soccer games and even taught his little brother how to ski—a skill that would serve Lolek well over the years; the sport would later overtake soccer as his favorite. His other developing passion, acting, was something Lolek could share with Mundek as well, and he performed some one-act plays for his brother's patients.

But a mere two years after Edmund's graduation from medical school, the dedicated doctor was dead. Edmund's gravestone would read that he had sacrificed his life by tending to victims of a scarlet fever outbreak in 1932.[14] He succumbed to the highly contagious disease at the age of twenty-six.

Lolek's neighbor Helen Szczepanksa had been a friend of Emilia's. Helen was saddened that the young boy had lost both his mother and his brother so early in life. When she expressed her sympathies, Lolek simply told her, "It was God's will." The faith in his statement surprised and impressed her. It was quite a mature attitude, she thought, from one thirty years younger than she.[15]

God provided other mentors for Lolek. In fact, throughout his young life there were both priests and laymen who took him under their wings and passed on their special knowledge to the quick yet humble student. These men provided him with shining examples of the dignity of the human person.

## MODEL PRIESTS

When Lolek was eleven he met the first of these men, Father Kazimierz Figlewicz. The priest arrived at Wadowice in 1930 to serve as vicar of St. Mary's Church. He trained the altar boys and taught catechism to the schoolchildren. Among those children was Lolek, whom Father Figlewicz discovered to be "very lively...very talented, very quick and very good."[16]

But what impressed the young priest most about the tall boy was the fervent way in which he served at the altar. The more the two ministered together, the more spiritually bonded they became. Soon the priest became the regular confessor and unofficial spiritual director to "my young and rather complicated soul," as Archbishop Wojtyla would later describe himself.[17]

When Father Figlewicz was transferred to the Wawel Cathedral at Kraków two years later, it was with great sadness that Lolek said good-bye. Through this parting, however, Lolek discovered another of his gifts, writing. He reported on the priest's departure for the *Sunday Bell*, Kraków's church paper.

Since Lolek was the president of the Altar Boys' Circle, he was given a full page in the children's section of the newspaper, "Little Bell." In his article Lolek not only quoted verbatim the farewell speech given by a weeping altar boy but also went on to describe vividly the sadness of all who were there, as well as the brief interlude of cheer the children experienced when they were served ice cream and chocolate.

Lolek and Father Figlewicz kept in touch with the occasional letter, and they met again when Lolek moved to Kraków. There Father Figlewicz would influence the young man even more and eventually enjoy the privilege of witnessing young Karol respond to the call to the priesthood.

Karol had other models to admire and follow, such as young Father Edward Zacher, the religious director of his school and a brilliant scientist. With doctorates in both science and theology, he taught religion classes in a special way, often deftly weaving the mysteries of science into the subject, creating lessons that were like tapestries depicting his awe for God's wondrous creation.

Father Zacher took note of Karol's intelligence. When he heard that the archbishop of Kraków would be coming to visit the parish of Wadowice, he knew exactly which student should give the welcoming address. Lolek accepted the assignment, although he felt unworthy to give the speech. As a humble secondary school student (albeit one who made straight As), he had never spoken before such a *"towering figure"* as the archbishop.[18]

Karol did such a good job, however, that Archbishop Adam Stefan Sapieha asked Father Zacher whether the young man might consider the priesthood. Father Zacher said that Karol planned to study Polish language and letters. "That's a pity," the archbishop replied.[19]

Archbishop Saphiea's disappointment was to be short-lived. He would later play a big role in helping to form Karol spiritually as a priest and eventually as his own successor as archbishop of Kraków.

## LANGUAGE AND LETTERS

Karol would next feed his interest in the words of man, which later inspired his love for the Word of God. His attention to Polish literature began in high school and blossomed into a deep love of the Polish language. This in turn led to an interest in all languages and finally to an intense appreciation of words themselves.

Karol expressed this passion in various ways: He wrote poetry, wrote and performed in plays, studied other languages whenever he could and participated in dramatic recitations and in other forms of public speaking. He immersed himself in the literature of Polish Romanticism and in the works of writers such as the Nobel Prize-winner Henryk Sienkiewicz, who wrote *Quo Vadis*; Adam Mickiewicz; Juliusz Slowacki and Cyprian Kamil Norwid.

It was during this time that he met his next mentor, Mieczyslaw Kotlarczyk. A history teacher in an all-girls school, Kotlarczyk was a "Wawro" whose father ran a local theater. He was also a devout Christian with a vision of what the art of drama could or even should be: a means of transmitting the spiritually intimate, the word within—God's Word. The theater was his church, and performances were his prayer. The dramas he directed were minimalist in production, and the spoken word—not the actor—was the star of the show.

Kotlarczyk's conviction in the primacy of the word struck the heart of sixteen-year-old Lolek, who became an apprentice of sorts to the twenty-eight-year-old teacher. Under Kotlarczyk's tutelage Lolek learned a strong, new way to give voice to what was in his soul. Pope John Paul II would later reflect on these days of his youth: "I inevitably drew closer to the mystery of the Word—that Word of which we speak every day in the *Angelus:* 'And the Word became flesh and dwelt among us' (Jn 1:14)."[20]

Among the female students at the school where Kotlarczyk taught history was Halina Królikiewicz. Her father, Jan, was the principal of the boys' school that Karol attended. Halina pursued the theater as much as Karol did, and she was often cast opposite him in productions. Over the years the two encouraged and challenged each other, even becoming friendly rivals at a poetry recitation competition.

The two teenagers must have been confident in their acting abilities, for they managed to secure a famous actress, Kazimiera Rychertowna, to be one of the judges of the contest. In the competition Karol recited Norwid's *Promethidion* with the quiet strength its words called for, but he still came in second to Halina's more dramatic performance.

Although Karol later would dance with Halina at their commencement ball, the two were only friends and were never romantically involved with each other. Remarkably studious and prayerful, Karol did not pursue romance, nor did he live the type of lifestyle that would lend itself to romance. Yet as pope, love would be the emotion that he would feel, understand and express more than any other, through his sermons, his writings and his contact with people. Over time the depth of his relationship with God would only increase, along with his love for all humanity.

## MOVE TO KRAKÓW

Not surprisingly, Karol was valedictorian at his high school graduation on May 27, 1938. He planned to follow in

Edmund's footsteps and enroll at Jagiellonian University. He would study philosophy.

But first, during the summer months that followed his graduation, Lolek had to serve in a youth paramilitary battalion, as was required of all young men his age. His assignment took him to the mountains south of Wadowice, where he helped to build a road. It was hard physical labor under the hot sun, but Lolek made friends while growing tan and strong.

That August he moved to Kraków with his father, so that in the fall he could walk easily to the university. Their new home was what a real estate agent might call "cozy." The apartment, in the basement of Number 10 Tyniecka Street, consisted of two rooms plus a kitchen and a bathroom.

The gray, two-story building had belonged to Lolek's bachelor uncle, Robert Kaczorowski, his mother's brother. Now his spinster sisters, Lolek's Aunt Rudolfa and Aunt Anna, occupied the upper floors. Even though Karol and his father were physically close to these family members, it does not appear that they were emotionally close to any of them; the basement dwellers lived a quiet, separate life from their family upstairs.

Lolek came to know his new town by visiting all sixty churches that dotted its street corners. One of these became his regular parish: the newly consecrated St. Stanislaw Koska, which was located on Konfederacka Street in Debniki and was a mere three-minute walk from home.

Once in school, Karol made many friends. He was the type of young man who commanded respect and admiration from others without intimidating them. He never set himself above anyone, yet his piety set him apart. There was something "extra" in it that even his classmates noticed. One day, as a joke, some of them pinned a card to his desk that read, "Karol Wojtyla—Apprentice Saint!"[21] It was not cruel teasing; on the contrary, it was a light-hearted way of recognizing the holiness in Karol that was apparent to all who knew him.

## ❦ 2 ❦

# Catholic Underground

KAROL ENJOYED HIS FIRST YEAR OF STUDY AT JAGIELLONIAN. But before he was able to start his second year, he found his university days brought to a sudden halt. The roar of airplanes over Poland on the morning of September 1, 1939, signaled the change in his life.

Although the German armies were advancing, Karol thought that there was perhaps still time to escape. The air raids had come in from the north, the south and the west, so he and his father joined the tens of thousands of Polish refugees streaming toward the east. The trek required much travel on foot, but sometimes the Wojtylas were able to secure a ride on a truck, a bus or even a horse cart.

The crossing was very wearying for Karol, Sr., and Lolek began to fear that his father wouldn't make it to the end.

Finally, after a more than ninety-mile journey, the Wojtylas turned back. Karol, Sr., was indeed worn out. Additionally, a secret pact made three weeks earlier between Moscow and Berlin allowed the Soviet Union to steamroll into Poland in a surprise invasion from the east, so there was nowhere left to run.[1]

## POLAND NO MORE

"The Pole has no rights whatsoever. His only obligation is to obey what we tell him." German Governor-General Hans Frank issued these words to his officers as he set up base in Kraków. He was plain about the Nazis' ultimate plan: "[Our] major goal…is to finish off as speedily as possible all trouble-making politicians, priests, and leaders.… [T]housands of so-called important Poles will have to pay with their lives… [and] the Polish nation is never again…to offer resistance. Every vestige of Polish culture is to be eliminated. The Poles…will work. They will eat little. And in the end they will die out. There will never again be a Poland."[2]

To outsiders this evil plan seemed to be working. By October 5 Nazi troops had marched victoriously into Warsaw as Adolf Hitler watched from a platform erected for the occasion. But by some miracle, the members of the Polish government had been able to escape into Romania. Poland never officially surrendered to Germany.

Although Poland would suffer the oppression, torture and great loss of life of its people over the next six years, the country would indeed survive, and without an army. It didn't need one. For even as the Nazis hung their red, white and black flags at Wawel Cathedral, underneath the flapping swastikas one could read the inscription over the doorway: "If God is for us, who can be against us?"

God's servants, however, would be major targets of the Nazis, who hoped to destroy Poland by attacking its culture. The Roman Catholic faith was a major aspect of Poland's identity, and no Catholic was safe. A priest could be shot for leading a procession around his own church or for hearing confession in Polish instead of in German.

Before the war was over, 5,000 priests and nuns would be sent to concentration camps, and nearly 3,000 of them would die there. A priest from Kraków, Father Piotr Dańkowski, died in Auschwitz with a log tied to his shoulders on Good Friday of 1942. Shortly afterward a Salesian, Father Józef Kowalski, would also die in Auschwitz, beaten and drowned in feces for refusing to grind his rosary beads under his foot.[3]

The last Mass Archbishop Sapieha was allowed to celebrate was on October 29, 1939. After that, he and the other priests and staff were officially turned out of the cathedral, with the exception of an elderly priest and Father Figlewicz. These two priests were allowed to celebrate Mass on Wednesday and Sunday mornings, as long as they were under German guard and no additional worshippers attended. Bit by bit the Nazis were trying to dismantle the Catholic Church.

Academia fared no better. In November 1939, when the SS called all professors and university staff members to a lecture at Jagiellonian, 184 academics showed up only to be ambushed by a Nazi squad. The soldiers entered Szujski Hall, arrested everyone and shipped them off to the Sachsenhausen concentration camp, where most of them would die.

By 1942 Jagiellonian University would rise from the ashes and continue to operate as a full university in secret. A faculty of 136 professors defiantly risked death by teaching 800 students in clandestine classes held in private homes.

Such intellectual stimulation was a great support to Lolek and in fact helped him maintain his sanity during that difficult time. He wrote to a friend: "I surround myself with books, I put up fortifications of Art and Learning. I work.... I read, write, learn, pray, and fight within myself. Sometimes I feel horrible pressure, sadness, depression, evil. Sometimes I almost glean the dawn...."[4]

Lolek also busied himself with a new favorite literary pursuit, playwriting. He wrote three plays in the year that followed, and as one can tell by their eponymous titles, they were versions of the biblical stories of David, Job and Jeremiah set during pivotal times in Polish history. *Job* was set in the present Nazi occupation. This modern Job suffered as much as the one in the scriptural version, and the play ended on the same notes of hope, resurrection and renewal.

## THE GIFT OF CARMEL

It is said that when the student is ready, the master appears. In Lolek's case it was Jan Leopold Tyranowski who arrived to mentor him. A deeply spiritual layman whom John Paul II would later describe as "really saintly,"[5] Tyranowski was trained as an accountant but chose to work as a clerk in his father's tailor shop on Rózana Street. This work provided him with quiet and contemplative moments in which he could develop his inner life.

The Salesian Fathers who ran the church in Debniki provided another way for Tyranowski to express his spirituality. The priests had run a few retreats for townspeople who were in their twenties and thirties. In order to build on the success of those gatherings, they hoped to start a prayer circle called "Living Rosary" for young people, and they needed someone to lead it. Tyranowski eagerly volunteered, and the Salesians accepted with gratitude, but there were some who questioned their decision. Tyranowski, it turned out, was not a popular figure in Debniki. In fact, he was generally looked upon as an odd and unpleasant person, being unattractive in appearance, awkward in expression and archaic in his catechism.

But the Living Rosary was given the green light, and Tyranowski vigorously stepped on the gas. His recruiting tactics left much to be desired. In his zeal to find members for the group, he would walk up to people and interrogate them on their spirituality. Surprisingly, this managed to pique the interest of enough people, including a friend of Karol, who then invited Karol to accompany him to a meeting one Saturday night. Accepting that invitation would change his life.

Tyranowski was immediately fond of Karol. And despite Tyranowski's ability to turn people off, Karol found himself drawn to the intensely spiritual man—perhaps because he was both prayerful and ascetic, like Karol's father. The young man hungrily received all the spirituality Tyranowski could give him. And give Tyranowski did.

Tyranowski met with Living Rosary members individually for counsel, basing his spiritual direction on the teachings of the Carmelite mystics Saint Teresa of Avila and Saint John of the Cross. Thanks to this influence, Carmelite spirituality would become the backbone of Karol's prayer life and would support him for the rest of his life.

The impact that Saints Teresa and John have had on the Roman Catholic Church is immeasurable. The Vatican recognized this by declaring them both "doctors of the Church." The two Spaniards were contemporaries—although Teresa was a good twenty years older than John—and lived at the time of the Inquisition. They knew each other personally and enjoyed a spiritual camaraderie, recognizing in each other the same call to lead the Carmelite order—and all Catholics, really—to a more intimate relationship with God through contemplative prayer. Indeed, they were the standard-bearers of a prayer renaissance, teaching that quiet recollection in the presence of God was the path all were called to follow, be one a priest, a monk or a layperson. Such prayer, they said, would nurture all aspects of a person's life.

Both saints wrote a number of books, but Karol was particularly inspired by the works of Saint John. This saint, when writing about contemplative prayer, was blessed with the ability to produce either a scholarly treatise or a deeply mystical poem. His most famous poem, "The Dark Night of the Soul," which was based on the love poetry of the Song of Songs, describes finding union with God even in the darkness of desolation.

Exposure to both this Spanish saint and his present-day Polish advocate affected Karol's soul to an immeasurable degree. In fact, Tyranowski's influence was so strong that years later Pope John Paul II admitted, "I don't know whether it is to him that I owe my priesthood calling, but...it was born within his climate."[6]

## A ROCK AMONG STONES

By the fall of 1940, all young Polish men were suspect to the Nazis. Those who were strong and healthy—and eventually even those who were not—were deported to Germany and forced to work in labor camps. In order to avoid that scenario, Karol had to find work in an industry that could be considered essential to the German war effort. He also needed to support himself and his father, as the Nazis had stopped payments of the lieutenant's pension. So the young Karol signed up to work at the Solvay chemical company's limestone quarry at Zakrzówek, which was only about a half-hour walk from where he lived in Debniki.

Throughout the bitter winter season, dressed in his "uniform" of oil-splashed and dust-caked denim, a jacket and large clogs, Karol made his daily descent into the pit for the backbreaking work of splitting calcinated rock. This rock was used to make caustic soda, which in turn was used to make explosives. The workday started early, and there was one fifteen-minute break for a breakfast that the workers were expected to provide for themselves. No lunch—neither the food nor the time to eat it—was provided.

Karol, his friend Juliusz Kydryński and the other students who worked with them managed to take turns sneaking off once or twice a day to warm themselves by the stove in the managers' hut. The managers were also Poles, and they recognized that many of their new workers were displaced university students who were not used to the hard physical labor of breaking up stone and shoveling it into small tramcars. Sympathetic to their plight, the managers often went out of their way to make the work easier if they could get away with it, such as reducing the quotas expected at the end of the workday.

Karol was not assigned the heaviest manual labor, and he was eventually made an assistant to Franciszek Labuś, the rock-blaster. This job carried a challenge all its own: working with dynamite. The danger of the explosive was made especially clear to Karol when he witnessed the death of one of his coworkers in a blast gone wrong. Karol watched as the dead body was laid out on the gravel and the man's wife called. He witnessed her frantic arrival at the quarry as well as the equally heartbreaking arrival of her son, who rushed over straight from school.

This coworker had been angry about the injustice of his situation in life. In fact, anger was ever-present at the quarry, pervading the air like so much dust. But Karol did not judge this emotion. He too was admittedly angry, but he could see beyond it to a deeper meaning. By working through the anger, he believed, a man could grow spiritually. He reflected about this time and again in his poetry of the period:

> The stone yields you its strength,
> and man matures through work
> which inspires him to difficult good.[7]

And

> ... [I]n man grows the equilibrium
> which love learns through anger.[8]

Karol saw everything not just with his physical eyes but also through the mystical lens of contemplative prayer. Contemplative prayer had become his weapon against bitterness;

it was the saving grace that would help him see beyond the obvious and offer him glimpses of the spiritual truths behind it. He would often record his insights in the form of poetry, as mystical understanding is not easily expressed in prose.

Without this prayer and poetry, Karol's deep anger at the unfairness of the war—and of the quarry work in particular— might have gotten the better of him. Instead he came to know, in a deeply personal way, the dignity of manual labor and of the human person made in the image of God. He grew in his appreciation of his coworkers—and of himself.

Karol also understood that the quarry was a training ground of sorts for him. He realized that he was there for a reason and that God could use this experience to make him a better man. Did he know that the Lord himself was mining a rock from that quarry—a rock upon which he would continue to build and fortify his Church? One poem hints at just that:

… [H]is own grandeur he does not know how to name.

No, not just hands drooping with the hammer's weight,
not the taut torso, muscles shaping their own style,
but thought informing his work,
deep, knotted in wrinkles on his brow,
and over his head, joined in a sharp arc, shoulders and
    veins vaulted.

So for a moment he is a Gothic building
cut by a vertical thought born in the eyes.
No, not a profile alone,
not a mere figure between God and the stone,
sentenced to grandeur and error.[9]

## ANOTHER SAD GOOD-BYE

Not long after Christmas 1940, Karol Wojtyla, Sr., became ill, so ill that in due time he was forced to take to his bed. Karol began taking his supper at the Kydryńskis' and then bringing food home for his father. On a bitterly cold February 18, he returned to the basement room on Tyniecka Street with dinner and medicine for his father. With him was Juliusz's sister Maria, who was going to help heat and serve the food. They found the elder Karol dead. A heart attack had taken him.

Karol wept bitterly at the scene, filled with regret at not having been there when his father passed away. Then he called a priest. He spent the rest of the night on his knees, praying before his father's body. On February 22, after a simple funeral, Karol Wojtyla, Sr., was buried at Rakowicki, Kraków's military cemetery.[10]

Not yet twenty-one, Karol was now alone in the world, and he felt the pain of it severely. At their invitation he moved in with the Kydryńskis, and he slept in the middle room of their three-room apartment. He would often be found lying on the floor, deep in prayer. In fact, prayer became his main source of comfort. Every day he attended Mass, and every day he visited his father's grave, where he prayed some more.

Later Pope John Paul II was able to look back on those days and marvel at how fortunate he was in comparison to others:

> *I was spared much* of the immense and horrible drama of the Second World War. I could have been arrested any day, at home, in the stone quarry, in the plant, and taken away to a concentration camp. Sometimes I would ask myself: so many young people of my own age are losing

their lives, *why not me?* Today I know that it was not mere chance. Amid the overwhelming evil of the war, everything in my own personal life was tending towards the good of my vocation. I cannot forget the kindnesses shown to me in that difficult period by people whom the Lord placed on my path.... [11]

One of the people the Lord placed in young Karol's path was Mieczyslaw Kotlarczyk, the founder of the Rhapsodic Theatre, who with his wife, Sofia, reentered Karol's life by moving into the former Wojtyla apartment. Karol later joined them, happy not to be alone under the roof where his father died.

The Kotlarczyks were like family to Karol. Mieczyslaw, in particular, would influence him greatly. He took day jobs, first as a tram driver and then as an office worker, but at night he engaged Karol in deep conversations about language and art and continued to train him in the recitation of the Word. Kotlarczyk's contribution to the formation of Pope John Paul II's public speaking skills cannot be underestimated. His direction helped form the presentation style of a man who would give speeches all over the world for over twenty-five years.

### GRANDMOTHER SZKOCKA

Another influential person was Irena Szkocka. Juliusz Kydryński brought Karol to her home one day, and the old woman and Karol were immediately taken with each other. Karol saw her as the grandmother he never really had, and she immediately saw something special in his bright yet modest manner.

Mrs. Szkocka had a lovely home at 55 Poniatowski Street called "Lime Tree Villa." It boasted a terrace with an enviable view of the Vistula River. Often Mrs. Szkocka would ask Juliusz and Karol over for a visit and would serve them from an elegant tea service as her daughter, Zofia, played Chopin on the piano. In their simple way of keeping up their customs, the charming mother-daughter team exercised formidable resistance to the Nazis' efforts to abolish all things culturally Polish, and they accomplished this simply by being themselves.

Karol began inviting Irena and Zofia to his home and to some of his performances with the revised Rhapsodic Theatre. So when the Nazis took a liking to the Szkocka home and commandeered it for themselves, Karol offered the use of his tiny flat to his friends. The unsinkable Irena found a place a few doors down from Karol's home instead, and having her so close by gave him great joy.

In true grandmotherly fashion, Mrs. Szkocka couldn't help but "adopt" all of Karol's friends, and soon his acting troupe found one of their regular meeting places in her home. They held some of their rehearsals in the largest room she had. Mrs. Szkocka, ever the hostess, prepared refreshments for them, and Zofia entertained them with music. Spiritual discussions would often bloom during rehearsals, and Mrs. Szkocka would listen with interest as Karol spoke enthusiastically about the depth he had discovered in the Carmelite way of prayer.

What Mrs. Szkocka didn't know was that Karol had seriously considered joining the Carmelites, even following his interest to the doorstep of the monastery of the Discalced

Carmelite Friars on Rakowicki Street. When he asked if they would accept him, they told him they could not, for the Carmelites were not taking any novices during wartime. The Germans, they knew, were hardly going to allow a young, intelligent man like Karol to stop working for them in the quarry and join a monastery. At best it would arouse suspicion; at worst it could mean death for the Carmelites and any young men they harbored. "Come again after the war," Karol was told.

## ACTOR OR PRIEST?

Karol continued his work in the Rhapsodic Theatre. During the occupation the group performed twenty-two times. This was in no way easy. In order to rehearse or perform, the actors had to make their way through the dark and dangerous streets of Kraków, dodging Nazi patrols that were hunting for curfew breakers such as themselves.

Most of the evening performances were the scenes and poems written by the greats of Polish literature. Karol was already familiar with many of these works, so his ability to focus on the meaning and power of the words was unrivaled. This became clear one dark night in November of 1942.

Karol was performing that evening in an adaptation of Adam Mickiewicz's classic of the Romantic Era, *Pan Tadeusz*. At one point when Karol was speaking, Nazi propaganda suddenly began blasting through a megaphone outside, rattling windows along with the nerves of the audience members. The only one apparently unaffected was Karol. Even though the audience could not hear him, they found themselves enraptured by his steadfast performance. Nothing would deter Karol from finishing what he had set out to do.

It was a scene that many would not forget, as it provided another glimpse as to what type of leader the future Pope John Paul II would be. Karol soon would reveal to his friends his discovery that his future did not lie in the theater:

> [A] light was beginning to shine ever more brightly in the back of my mind: *the Lord wants me to become a priest.* One day I saw this with great clarity: it was like an interior illumination which brought with it the joy and certainty of a new vocation. And this awareness filled me with great inner peace.[12]

Karol discussed his decision with Father Figlewicz, who secretly submitted his name to Archbishop Sapieha. Karol would be one of ten applicants to be accepted. And thus the Rhapsodic Theatre came to lose one of its star performers.

Even though Kotlarczyk was a devout Catholic, he fought Karol's newfound vocation. He believed that Karol already had a true calling in theater, and he could not bear the thought of losing his protégé. Karol's fellow actors, including his old friend Halina, also had a difficult time understanding his decision. Tadeusz Kudliński held an all-night debate with Karol about the matter—risking arrest for breaking curfew. But Karol was decided and would not budge.

## SECRET SEMINARIAN

In the Nazis' continued fight against higher education, they had ordered Polish seminaries to replace their university-level instructors with trade school–type teachers. When the Church ignored this directive, the Nazis forbade new aspirants from entering the seminary at all. Ordinations were strictly forbidden.

Ever ready to parry, Archbishop Sapieha countered by cleverly disguising his future priests as newly hired secretaries and then assigning them to various local parishes. He also developed a secret underground seminary, with classes at odd hours and in unconventional places. Times being as dangerous as they were, the seminarians were not even told who else was in "school" with them.

Some underground seminarians were captured in raids and subsequently sent to concentration camps or shot by the Gestapo. Karol was saddened when he learned that Jerzy Zachuta, a friend with whom he had often served Mass, had been taken from his home and executed by a Nazi firing squad.

Karol suffered his own brush with death during this time. It was on a February afternoon in 1944, when he was making his way home after working two shifts back-to-back at the Solvay plant. His route was a long one, and it required that he walk along the edge of a road. In his fatigue he failed to hear a German army truck coming up behind him. It is not clear if the driver of the vehicle saw Karol, but he certainly did not honk his horn in warning. Karol only became aware of the truck when its hood struck his body. He fell down, hit his head against the edge of the sidewalk and lost consciousness. The Nazis continued on their way.

Karol lay there with his head and face covered in blood, losing precious body heat with each passing minute and gradually slipping into shock. It would be many hours before Józefa Florek, riding a nearly empty tram down the lonely street, noticed his crumpled form lying by the side of the road and rushed to his aid.

Seeing the injured Karol, a German officer driving by in a command car pulled over to investigate, and after assessing the situation, ordered the driver of a passing lumber truck to drop the injured man off at the Kopernik Street Hospital. Diagnosed with a concussion, Karol was admitted to the hospital for a two-week stay. After his release he was ordered to continue his convalescence for another few weeks at home. His "grandmother," Irena Szkocka, took him in and nursed him back to health.[13]

## BLACK SUNDAY

August 1944 began with a bang called the Great Warsaw Uprising. Not to be confused with the Warsaw Ghetto Uprising, which was a brave but futile resistance effort by approximately 700 Jews, the Warsaw Uprising was a larger battle that took place in greater Warsaw. The homegrown army of 38,000 Poles made a valiant effort, but after a sixty-three-day struggle, they were also unsuccessful, suffering great loss of life in the process.

The Germans lost a good number of soldiers too, approximately 16,000. Even though the Nazis technically "won" the battle, they knew they couldn't afford to suffer similar losses if any other Polish cities decided to follow Warsaw's lead. They began a sweep of each city to remove all potential resistance elements.

On August 6 the Nazis swarmed into Kraków. They canvassed each neighborhood, street by street, building by building, breaking into homes and dragging men and boys away from their families. Some 8,000 men and boys would be abducted in this roundup; some would return, others would never be seen again. It was a dark day in the history of Kraków, and it was known ever after as "Black Sunday."

Karol was at home with the Kotlarczyks when the Nazis turned down Tyniecka Street. Mrs. Kotlarczyk grew hysterical, and she repeatedly urged her husband to hide in the bushes in the garden outside. Paralyzed with fright, Mr. Kotlarczyk stayed where he was, sitting at the table. Karol's response to the threat was to fall to his knees and pray.

When the Nazis finally broke into the home, they prowled through the first floor and then the second. Then they left, ignoring the basement apartment altogether. Mrs. Kotlarczyk could barely believe it. *How did they miss us?* she wondered. Then she saw Karol, still kneeling on the floor and praying.

Archbishop Sapieha decided that for safety's sake his class, now reduced to seven men, should live with him in his palace, disguised as ordained priests. He would finish educating them there himself. A priest came to fetch Karol. In order to avoid suspicion, his "Grandmother" Szkocka walked with them to the residence on Franciszkańska Street. There Karol would remain until the end of the war a few months later.

## VENI, CREATOR SPIRITUS

There was not much celebration when the Germans fled Kraków on the night of January 17, 1945, as with the morning came the Communists, who quickly took over. One fortunate result of this change, however, was that although the Communists wished to make Poland an atheist country, the seminary no longer had to conduct itself in secret. It officially became part of Jagiellonian University again.

Soon afterward Sapieha was named a cardinal, and it was as Cardinal Sapieha that he singled Karol out for early ordination. He wished to send his star pupil to study at the Angelicum—Rome's most prestigious school of theology—rather than immediately assign him to a parish. Classes would begin there soon.

And so it was that in the fall of 1946 Karol found himself lying facedown on the floor of the private chapel of the archbishop of Kraków, his forehead against the cool of the tiles, his arms outstretched on either side of him in the form of the cross, listening to a choir singing the prayer for the Holy Spirit to come upon him:

*Veni, Creator Spiritus,*
*mentes tuorum visita,*
*Imple superna gratia*
*quae tu creasti pectora.*

They then sang the names of saints—martyrs, confessors, popes and virgins—and pleaded for their intercession.

When Karol arose, it was only to kneel as Cardinal Sapieha laid his hands on his head and ordained him a priest of the Roman Catholic Church. It was November 1, the Feast of All Saints.

# ❊ 3 ❊

## *The Church's Servant*

AFTER TAKING A BUS TO GDÓW AND THEN AN OXCART to Marszowice, Father Karol Wojtyla hiked the rest of the way to his first parish assignment in Niegowić, past waving fields of grain. When he finally made it onto the parish property, the new priest knelt down and kissed the ground.

It was 1948. Father Wojtyla had just returned from Rome, where he had passed his doctoral examinations with a perfect score. His dissertation had been on Saint John of the Cross and the Carmelite's "doctrine of faith." Now, after two years of studying mysticism and the most profound ideas of philosophy, he was assigned to "a small parish at the end of the world."[1]

There was no electricity or running water in the priest's house, although there was a well nearby. Out back a kitchen garden and chickens provided some staples for regular meals. Completing the bucolic picture was a nearby orchard and a collection of lime trees in the front. Poverty was nothing new to Father Wojtyla, and he settled easily into his new home.

Although Poland's situation had improved somewhat, the country was still under the gun of a foreign army, and sometimes it appeared as if only the uniforms had changed. One of the first orders of business for the Soviets had been to exterminate thousands of Poles whom they had falsely accused of collaborating with the Nazis. Then they commandeered the Nazi concentration camps and converted them— with very little effort—into labor camps. Judeo-Christian religion was still suspect in Poland, and the Jewish people in particular were still singled out for mistreatment. The war was over in most of the world, but Poland would not be free for many years.

Nevertheless, it pleased Karol to be home. He would serve in Niegowić for just eight months. Cardinal Sapieha— and the Lord Jesus—had other things in mind for him.

## A Modern Job

One who had not lived to see Karol's return to Poland was Jan Tyranowski, his spiritual director and mentor in Carmelite contemplative prayer. While Karol was in school, Tyranowski had contracted an infection that left him bedridden and racked with pain. Seeing in his suffering an opportunity to mortify his flesh, he received concerned visitors with a patient smile.

Tyranowski did not complain even when he began to have trouble with his hand and had to be admitted to the hospital. When his arm swelled in size and his doctors prescribed painkillers, he refused to take them. He believed that suffering had spiritual value, and rather than simply wait for the new medicine called penicillin to arrive from overseas, he wished to experience his suffering and offer it up for the good of others—most especially for those in the seminary and for Karol in particular.

Tyranowski endured constant, agonizing pain for an entire year, remaining serene through it all. He was comforted at times by letters from Karol which, after reading, he would clutch to his chest. Karol would address him in the letters as "Job," after the long-suffering character in Scripture. Tyranowski's spiritual stamina moved Karol to ask "Grandmother" Szkocka to "pray that I may, to the best of my ability, become an imitator of Christ and of those who reflect him so perfectly."[2] By "those," Mrs. Szkocka surmised, Karol meant Tyranowski.

Although the penicillin eventually arrived, it was too late to have any effect. Tyranowski's condition worsened, and eventually he had to have his arm amputated. This was followed by complete hearing loss and, finally, his death in March 1947 at the age of forty-six.

> But the souls of the righteous are in the hand of God,
> and no torment will ever touch them.
> . . .
> [T]hey are at peace.
> For though in the sight of men they were punished,
> their hope is full of immortality.
> Having been disciplined a little, they will receive great
> good,

> because God tested them and found them worthy of
> himself;
> like gold in the furnace he tried them,
>     and like a sacrificial burnt offering he accepted
>     them. (Wisdom 3:1, 3–6)

## MUSIC MAN

A new happiness entered Father Wojtyla's life in 1949, when he was assigned to St. Florian, a church in his familiar Kraków. The parish included a large number of university students, and it was there that he began the youth ministry that would prove to be very close to his heart. The giant World Youth Days and other youth rallies he led as pope would have their beginnings in his "little family" (or *Rodzínka*), a tiny seed planted in 1951.

Father Wojtyla first recruited young people through music. He loved to sing, and he was often told he had a nice voice. So on the first evening of February 1951, he approached a few young women from the university and invited them to come the following evening to help form a choir.

The next night, the Feast of the Presentation of the Child Jesus in the Temple, the women found the young mysterious priest waiting for them in the shadows of the choir loft. Although he was shabbily dressed and they didn't even know his name, there was something about the unassuming figure that they trusted. In no time at all he had them assembled, and as it was the last day of the season to sing Christmas carols, he started with a few.

The priest next led the women in arrangements of Gregorian chant. The practice went well, and he asked the young women to return in the morning for the 6:00 Mass. They would sing with the young men from Kraków Polytechnic whom he had also recruited.

The group became a regular choir of almost twenty people, and singing at the 6:00 AM Wednesday Mass became their weekly event. The experience of meeting on a regular basis in the spirit of cooperation and community was very appealing to them, as were the stimulating intellectual and spiritual dialogues that began to bloom from their get-togethers. Soon groups began meeting on a regular basis on Thursday evenings in one another's homes to exchange ideas on philosophical subjects. Their dialogues were mediated by the priest they nicknamed "Sadok," after an enigmatic priest character of Polish literature.

Even after they learned Father Karol Wojtyla's real name, they didn't use it much. He became an uncle figure to the young people. And that's what they called him: "Uncle," or "Wujek." Although the title was an affectionate term, it was also a necessary one. The Communists forbade Catholics from congregating and worshiping in public. If Karol were identified as a priest while he was with a group, they would all be in danger of being arrested. So when they went out, "Father" would dress up in his hiking clothes and become "Uncle."

The group would take a train out of the city and enjoy a day in the woods, picnicking, boating—and receiving the Eucharist in a secret Mass. Borrowing from the minimalist style of his Rhapsodic Theatre days, "Uncle" would create a chapel in the woods by tying two oars together in the shape of a cross and planting it in the ground. Then he would turn over his kayak to create a makeshift altar.

Wujek's "family" became a sort of resistance group. Together they were free. They could worship as they pleased and discuss whatever they liked without censure. They prayed together, celebrated together and served the needy in their parish together. And as they had begun as a choir that sang at the Eucharist, their other activities often revolved around sacramental celebrations. Many of them eventually married other members of the group, the weddings celebrated by their "uncle-father" and their children baptized by him as well.

The priest encouraged the students to recruit more members, so the group continued to grow in number. What started as a "little family" became a *Srodowisko* ("milieu"), numbering 200. The group would separate into smaller groups for intellectual conversation. One of these named itself *Paczka,* the Polish word for "packet" or "small parcel."

## THE PROFESSOR

Cardinal Sapieha's death on July 23, 1951, was like the passing of a family member, not only for Father Karol but for all of Kraków. Thousands of people paid their final respects and prayed by his body, which lay in a coffin surrounded by candles in Wawel Cathedral. The cardinal had been a light during the dark years of both Nazi and Communist occupation, and people grieved that this light had gone out.

Sapieha's successor, Archbishop Baziak, advised Karol to go back to school for two more years so that he could earn a second doctorate and qualify to teach at a university. Although Karol preferred to stay with his parish (and he would continue to do pastoral work with his "family" from St.

Florian's), he obeyed the archbishop's direction. And so it was that in 1954, on top of his doctorate of theology, Father Wojtyla became a doctor of ethics. His thesis was on the phenomenologist Max Scheler. Perhaps it was these studies that moved him to earn his third doctorate—this time in philosophy—in 1957.

Phenomonology is a branch of philosophy that brings the science of the head into the physical presence of the hand, so to speak. It is a holistic approach, a way of examining the human experience from many angles and understanding how the emotional, physical and spiritual are united, connected and influenced by one another. Karol used phenomonology as a way of explaining ethics and the reality, meaning and importance of morality. Morality, he believed, is not a learned set of behaviors but the truth about how we are structurally made to be. Therefore, moral choices and actions are what give people the most emotional, spiritual and physical—that is to say, complete—satisfaction.

After achieving his second doctorate, Karol was assigned to the philosophy department of the Catholic University of Lublin. Still young and poorly dressed, Professor Wojtyla stood out among the professors as someone more interested in the deepest questions of life than in the material world—or in grades and footnotes, for that matter. More often than not, instead of an hour lecture on one subject, his class was more like philosophy classes of classical times. Although Wojtyla could certainly speak on one idea for a long period of time when he was so inspired, he did not lord over his students but instead engaged them in debates and discussions. He respected the ideas of others; he listened as well as he spoke.

His friend Father Mieczyslaw Maliński visited his classroom on more than one occasion in order to get an idea of Karol's teaching style.

> [He] generally began on a light, humorous note and then passed without effort to the deepest analyses, observations and deductions, summarizing existing material and transforming it into a coherent whole.... Karol was not concerned merely with emotions and experiences but with the whole of human personality, including will and intellect as well as feeling. The more I listened to him, however, the more I realized that he was presentng his own philosophy of mankind and not just that of St. Thomas, Scheler [or other philosophers]. Elements of his thinking might be traced to one or another of those great minds, but it was a personal philosophy and not simply an eclectic one. He was always keenly interested in human personality.... Above all he was interested in the supreme experience which is love—both love in general... and particular forms of it such as married love.[3]

As with his "little family," Father Wojtyla would sometimes teach his doctoral students out in the woods, on hiking trails or boating trips. Classes could be vacations, and vacations, classes. He began to bring along drafts of what would become his first book, *Love and Responsibility*, and ask the group to go over it and let him know what they thought.

One of the major themes of Wojtyla's spirituality was the dignity of the human person. He strongly believed that because everyone was created in the image of God, everyone had the right to live: the unborn, the sick, the elderly, minorities, the disabled and so on. This meant too that everyone was responsible for treating one another and the earth around them with respect.

*Love and Responsibility* focuses on the sexual side of this issue. The book uses science, psychology, Scripture and Church doctrine to show that a full understanding of the gift of sexuality leads to a tremendous reverence for it and a better understanding of the meaning of life as a whole. These themes would play key roles throughout Karol Wojtyla's ministry.[4]

## TWO DELIVERIES

Karol went on a two-week kayaking trip on the River Lyne with a small group in August of 1958. He was concerned that he wouldn't be able to hear from his friends Stanislaw and Danuta Rybicki, who were expecting the birth of their first child. He wanted to know when the happy event took place. Fortunately, Karol and his fellow vacationers were able to have their mail forwarded to them at rest stops along the river.

A few days into their journey, a son—Stanislaw, Jr.,—was born to his friends. But when Karol picked up his mail, it was not a birth announcement he found but rather a summons to the office of Cardinal Stefan Wyszyński in Warsaw.

After hitching a ride on the back of a passing milk truck and ducking into a public restroom to make a quick change, Karol stepped back into the sun looking again like Father Wojtyla. And that is how he presented himself before the cardinal. Wyszyński in turn informed him that Pope Pius XII had just named Karol titular bishop of Ombi and auxiliary to Archbishop Eugeniusz Baziak, apostolic administrator of the archdiocese of Kraków.

Although Karol accepted the nomination of bishop, he did so with reluctance. He was only thirty-eight years old, and perhaps he felt unworthy of such an honor at his age. Or perhaps he foresaw something of his future in St. Peter's Square. Whatever his concerns were, they drove him to search for a place in which to pray over the news privately.

He found the answer to his hopes in an Ursuline convent in town. Allowed inside because he was wearing a cassock, Karol was led by one of the sisters to the chapel and left there alone to pray before the Blessed Sacrament. Later, when a nun entered the chapel to guide the guest out, she found him lying prostrate on the floor, taking the position he had assumed at his ordination Mass. Struck by the dramatic sight, she tiptoed out, wondering if he wasn't atoning for sins in some way.

A while later the sister returned to invite him to supper, but she found him still lying facedown on the floor. He asked her to allow him to stay. "My train for Kraków doesn't leave until midnight. Allow me to stay. I have a lot to discuss with the Lord."[5]

The visiting priest was allowed to finish his prayer time. Soon after that he was kayaking with his friends again, giving them the news that their "Uncle-Father" would soon be "Uncle-Bishop."

## TOTUS TUUS

Wujek became Bishop Karol Wojtyla, successor to the apostles, on September 28, 1958. It was a wet and overcast day, but the bad weather could not keep away Karol's supporters.

45

They watched in awe as the entire crown of his head was anointed with the holy oil called chrism. As its sweet perfume permeated the air, Archbishop Baziak prayed over him, asking God to keep the new bishop untiring, fervent and humble. The archbishop also asked God to strengthen Karol to cherish the truth always and not be turned by flattery or overpowered by fear. It was a prayer that was heard to its last syllable.

As the arched hat called the bishop's mitre was placed on the kneeling Karol Wojtyla's head, the sun suddenly shone through the stained-glass windows above the altar. With apparent divine timing, light streamed down and bathed the new bishop in its radiance.[6]

A new bishop in the Roman Catholic Church gets to design a coat of arms and choose a motto to help define his episcopate. In order to offer the Virgin Mary all the graces he would receive as a bishop and to thus consecrate himself to Christ through her, Bishop Wojtyla chose the phrase *Totus Tuus*—"Totally Yours"—as his motto. He took his inspiration from a prayer of that name by Louis de Montfort: *Totus tuus ego sum, et omnia mea tua sunt, O Virgo, super omnia benedicta.* The English translation reads: "I am all yours, and all that is mine is yours, O Virgin, blessed above all."[7]

Bishop Wojtyla asked that his shield be a vivid shade of blue to represent the mantle of the Blessed Mother. He had it overlaid with the simple graphic of a golden yellow cross. And for the final touch, on the lower right-hand corner of the shield a large letter *M* was inscribed to symbolize Mary at the foot of the cross.

Bishop Wojtyla took his new job as a leader of the

Church very seriously. One of his first projects grew into a decades-long struggle—the battle for Nowa Huta.

Nowa Huta was a new town outside of Kraków, designed by the Communists to be a "model workers' town." It had been built without a church, a shameful first in the history of Poland. Bishop Wojtyla wouldn't let it be a town without a Christmas, however. He daringly staged an open-air Mass in the town on Christmas Eve, 1959. Although it was a bitterly cold night, a good number of the faithful showed up. And thus began a Christmas tradition, much to the chagrin of the Communist party.[8]

Although no one is sure why, on the ninth year of the Christmas Eve Mass, the Communists gave in and agreed to the construction of a church. It would take ten years to complete the building. Bishop Wojtyla supplied the first stone for its foundation—a rock from St. Peter's Basilica, a gift from Pope Paul VI.

## AT THE SEMINARY OF THE HOLY SPIRIT

Meanwhile Cardinal Angelo Giuseppe Roncalli had become Pope John XXIII, and he began shaking the foundations of the Church by calling for an ecumenical council. Such councils are rarely convened and are very important when they are. They are named after the places they are held, such as the Council of Trent and the Council of Nicaea. This new council would be called "Vatican II," as it would be the second council held at the Vatican.

The pope summoned theologians and Church dignitaries from their papal appointments at cathedrals, colleges and religious chapters around the world. These would come together at St. Peter's Basilica and follow a legal procedure in discussing, debating and voting on certain Church teachings, doctrines and practices. Their final decisions would become official decrees for the entire Church. These decisions would require a lot of preparation to make and years of work to see through.

Previous popes had called councils for the purposes of defining and declaring official tenets of the Church through the intercession of the Holy Spirit. This particular council wasn't so much about establishing new dogma as it was about freshening established dogma, updating it for modern times. There were issues in medicine, technology and ecumenical and international relations that had not been concerns during the previous council ninety years before. These plainly needed to be addressed. The goal was a renewal of the Church so that, in the words of Pope John XXIII, it could further "radiate before all...the lovable features of Jesus Christ, who shines in our hearts that God's splendor may be revealed."9

Every bishop in the Roman Catholic Church was allowed to vote at the council. In the spirit of disclosure, representatives of other Christian churches, together with some non-voting Catholics, were invited to sit in on the proceedings. The final turnout was impressive: 85 cardinals, 8 patriarchs, 533 archbishops, 2,131 bishops, 12 abbots, 14 prelates *nullius* and 67 heads of orders and congregations.10

Bishop Wojtyla was very excited to take part in what he knew would be a historic event in the history of the Church and certainly one of the most important events to occur in the twentieth century. Mystic that he was, he saw the event through spiritual eyes, calling what transpired there "the seminary of the Holy Spirit."[11] He made sure to attend each of the four two-month-long sessions.

These sessions took place over a three-year period, beginning on October 11, 1962, and ending on December 8, 1965. When Pope John XXIII died in June 1963, Pope Paul VI took up the reins and, with quiet efficiency, made sure the council continued to its natural end.

## BUILDING THE CHURCH

Wojtyla became well acquainted with his chair at the council. It was located somewhere in the middle of one of the two walls of stadium-type seating that ran the length of St. Peter's Basilica. There were a desk and a kneeler for each participant, assigned according to rank and age. Nearby were two refreshment stands, dubbed Bar Mitzvah and Bar Jonah, where coffee could be ordered. Karol enjoyed a good cappuccino.

Each morning the Church leaders would celebrate Mass, call upon the Holy Spirit to guide them and then get to work. For the next few hours those who were scheduled to give presentations would talk on specific subjects—in Latin. The session would officially end by noon, and then the larger group would disperse into smaller groups, where discussion and debate went on for the rest of the afternoon.

The dialogues taking place among bishops and others might never have happened had it not been for the council. Often Wojtyla appeared to be taking notes, some of which, he would later admit, were for a book that he was writing.

However, blessed with a phenomenal memory, he could easily recall the points made at every presentation.

During the Christmas break of 1963, a number of the bishops, at the urging of Pope Paul VI, traveled together to the Holy Land. Bishop Wojtyla was one of them. They found renewal as they walked in the steps of the apostles.

One stop that particularly struck Wojtyla was the Temple Mount in Jerusalem. There had stood the great temple of the one true God, what Jesus had referred to as "my Father's house" (Luke 2:49). The bishop may have connected it to St. Peter's Basilica, where the modern-day apostles were calling upon the Holy Spirit for guidance on how to continue to build the Church within the soul of each human being.

Back at the council Bishop Wojtyla spoke twice about how to better build the Church. His first talk was on religious freedom, an issue that was being hotly debated at the time. Unfortunately, he spoke from a philosophical viewpoint and hadn't developed his idea enough to get his point across very well. He knew this, but he felt it was important for him to speak up. As he later told his longtime friend Father Mieczyslaw Maliński, he thought "the main theme of the whole Council" should really be "the dignity of the human person and humanity in general."[12]

In his second talk, on the Church in the world, the bishop was better able to express his original ideas. He explained that the Church, which possesses the whole truth, should not expect the world to believe and thus follow the truth. Rather, the Church should help the world discover the truth, recognize it and accept it. Evangelization is not accomplished through moralizing or through a clerical attitude of superiority but through respect for the creatures God has made in his own image.

## THE ARCHBISHOP

Near the end of Vatican II Bishop Wojtyla received the news that he had been appointed archbishop of Kraków. His investiture must have touched him very deeply. He was returning to the cathedral in Kraków as its shepherd, to follow in the footsteps of Archbishop Sapieha and of Saint Stanislaw—martyr, patron of Poland and personal hero of Wojtyla.

In the courtyard the archbishop-elect received the relics of the great saint and kissed the ground. He ascended the steps of the cathedral and then was handed its keys. Entering through the main door, he processed to resounding organ music up the main aisle toward the sanctuary, under the grand yet familiar vaulted ceilings. He stopped to pray at the tomb of his beloved Saint Stanislaw. Continuing past the tomb of Queen Jadwiga, he knelt reverently before the Blessed Sacrament. Finally he sat on the provisional throne on the main altar.

The appointment from Pope Paul VI was read aloud, stating in part:

> There are in Poland not a few dioceses deserving special praise, among them the metropolitan see of Cracow....
> [T]his see has always been of such importance and dignity that the choice of an archbishop and supreme pastor has not only required earnest thought but has been to us a source of great joy: for it will provide the sheep of that numerous flock with a shepherd, leader and teacher thanks to whose wisdom they can advance in holiness.[13]

Then it came time for the new archbishop to speak:

> [T]oday... I feel above all the sense of something being
> born.... I wish to pay the deepest worship... of which I
> myself am capable... to the Eternal Word, the Son born
> eternally of the Father.... The life which God's Son has
> given us... reflects his own eternal sonship within the
> Holy Trinity—that life he has also bestowed upon our
> mother the Church.... And I look on this solemnity of
> my enthronement today as a new birthday in God, in
> Christ and in the Church.[14]

In 1963, during a break in the council sessions, Wojtyla had
ordained Stanislaw Dziwisz a priest. Three years later
Archbishop Wojtyla saw in Dziwisz someone who could
help him with his administrative duties. He hired the young
priest as a chaplain, and a new friendship was born. Dziwisz
showed himself to be so trustworthy, helpful and efficient
that Wojtyla would promote him to the position of principal secretary—that is, Wojtyla's right-hand man. It would
be a position that Dziwisz would maintain for the rest of
Wojtyla's life.

When the new archbishop returned to Rome, he was
reunited with Jerzy Kluger, his former Jewish schoolmate and
fellow soccer player. The two had not seen each other since
the beginning of World War II. Kluger, an engineer working
in Rome, had read in the newspaper Wojtyla's speech on the
Church in the world, and thus he had come to know that an
Archbishop Karol Wojtyla from Kraków was attending the
council.

## A Freshman in the College

When Archbishop Wojtyla was only forty-seven years old, Pope Paul VI made him the youngest cardinal in the Catholic Church. This honor gave him a ranking in the Church that was second only to that of the pope. It also gave him the right to vote in papal elections.

One of Wojtyla's first acts as cardinal was to order the restoration of Wawel Cathedral, the seat of both Saint Stanislaw and Cardinal Stefan Sapieha. Over 600 years old and containing the graves of kings and queens, the church had suffered damage during the Nazi occupation.[15]

Wojtyla also visited the synagogue in Kazimierz, the Jewish district of Kraków, the first cardinal in the history of Poland to do so. After conversing with some rabbis, he was allowed inside. He stood in the back and respectfully listened to the service.[16]

The cardinal was not only pioneering but brave and wise. His priests knew they could come to him with their troubles. One priest was being harassed by the Communist government for unpaid taxes. Imposing ridiculously large dues on parishes was another way the regime found to shut down churches or at least make their presence "worth something."

The scared and burdened priest simply couldn't afford to pay the taxes. He asked the cardinal what he should do. Cardinal Wojtyla gave him surprising advice: Go to jail. Once the priest turned himself in to the authorities, the cardinal assured him, everything would be taken care of.

The priest obeyed his superior and reported for imprisonment. Meanwhile, Cardinal Wojtyla showed up at the priest's church. As thousands gathered to hear him, he announced that their pastor was in jail for not paying the taxes. Further, the cardinal said, he would be taking over for the priest while he was away. The priest was quickly released.[17]

On another occasion the cardinal was greatly displeased when an assistant pastor committed a "serious misdemeanor." He called the young priest into his office and admonished him for a lengthy period of time, then he led the shaken priest into the chapel to pray. After they knelt together in silence for another long period, the cardinal slowly stood up and asked the young priest to hear his confession.[18]

"Is it becoming for a cardinal to ski?" someone once asked Karol.

"It is unbecoming for a cardinal to ski badly," Karol replied.

For the Communists, however, it seems it was unbecoming for a cardinal to ski at all. One day, while he was skiing in the Tatras, Cardinal Wojtyla accidentally crossed the Czechoslovakian border. The border patrol stopped him and demanded his identity papers. A look at his list of titles convinced the militiaman that the skier had moronically stolen the identity papers of someone important. When the cardinal insisted that he was the man his papers said he was, the office scoffed. "A skiing cardinal? Do you think I'm crazy?"[19] He took Wojtyla in for questioning.

A few phone calls confirmed the truth. "You should know…that half of the Polish cardinals ski," Karol explained at the command post.[20] There were only two Polish cardinals in the Church.

## THE DEATH OF THE SHEPHERD

The summer residence of the pope is in a small town southeast of Rome called Castel Gandolfo. Essentially a palace, the residence was designed by Carlo Maderno and built for Pope Urban VIII on the ruins of a villa once belonging to the Roman emperor Domitian. It boasts nearly four centuries' worth of some of the finest architecture and art Italy has to offer. The reception hall alone is a showplace of stunning marble, magnificent tapestries and ornate, hand-painted display panels.

All of the popes who have resided there have added to its splendor in one way or another. One of Pope Paul VI's additions was a painting in the chapel. Interestingly enough, it is a painting of Poland's "Luminous Mountain"—Jasna Góra—being protected by Our Lady of Czestochowa against the Swedish invasion of 1655. After having it installed, Pope Paul VI looked it over and pronounced prophetically, "It will serve my successor!"[21]

Sadly, it was at Castel Gandolfo that Pope Paul VI died of a massive heart attack on August 6, 1978, at 9:41 PM. At that moment the travel alarm clock that he had brought with him everywhere he went for nearly six decades inexplicably went off. It was a clock he had purchased in Poland.[22]

# ❧ 4 ❧

## *Habemus Papam!*

THE END OF POPE PAUL VI'S REIGN BEGAN THE CHAIN OF events that marked 1978 as "The Year of Three Popes." In September, over 100 cardinals descended upon St. Peter's Basilica to vote for his successor.

Many people would consider Karol Cardinal Wojtyla's election to the papacy a complete surprise. Perhaps in Rome, where the media like to keep up with who is *papabile* (which quite literally means "popeable"), his election was even shocking. After all, there hadn't been a non-Italian pope elected in over 400 years, the idea being that the bishop of the diocese of Rome should be a "local boy." Further, there had never been a pope from long-suffering Poland.

Yet a quick look back at Wojtyla's life shows us hints of what was to come. Among those who foresaw his eventual ascension to the papal chair were a poet, an elderly lady, a saint, a small child, a Harvard University student and two old friends.

PROPHECIES

> Amid discord the Lord God strikes
> An immense bell,
> Behold, for a Slavic pope
> He opens a throne.
> This one will not flee before swords
>
> …
>
> He is daring, like God, he goes to the sword:
> The world to him is powder!
>
> His face is radiant with the Word,
> A lamp for the servant
>
> …
>
> Thus, here comes a Slavic pope,
> A brother of the people[1]

The great Polish mystic Juliusz Slowacki wrote these words in the 1800s. Karol had recited this poet's works often in his days in the Rhapsodic Theatre. But had he ever entertained the notion that this poem was possibly a prophecy about him?

Even if he hadn't, others had. His adopted "grandmother," Irena Szkocka, read those lines and the following ones in her copy of Slowacki's poems:

> He will sweep out the churches and make them clean
>     within,
> God shall be revealed, clear as day, in the creative world.

Mrs. Szkocka wrote in the margin, "This Pope will be Karol."[2] Unfortunately, she didn't live to see her words come true, for she died in 1971 at the age of ninety-two.

In 1947 another mystic, Padre Pio, the great Italian Capuchin monk who bore the wounds of Christ on his person and whom Pope John Paul II would later canonize, also may have had a revelation about Wojtyla's future. It is said that when the young Father Karol was touring Italy, he went to Padre Pio for confession. After absolving him, Padre Pio is said to have told him that one day he would be dressed in white as the successor to the chair of Saint Peter.[3]

Then there was the little girl from Ludzmierz who welcomed him on his return to Kraków six weeks after he was appointed cardinal. She read a poem that ended with the anticipation that his next promotion would be to the papacy. While adults around them laughed, Cardinal Wojtyla did not. Respecting the dignity and the sincerity of the little girl—and perhaps quietly mulling over her innocent prophecy—he leaned down and gave her a kiss on the forehead.[4]

A Harvard University student seems to have had a flash of divine insight about Cardinal Wojtyla. In 1976 he heard the cardinal give a talk on the campus called "Alienation or Participation?" When reporting on it afterward, underneath a photo of the cardinal he wrote the caption, "A probable successor to Paul VI."[5]

Professor Stefan Swiezawski was enlightened with an understanding of Cardinal Wojtyla's future one day in 1974. He had been friends with Karol for twenty-five years, but that afternoon, after hearing the cardinal give a reflection on Saint Thomas during a retreat near Rome, the startling revelation came to him: Karol would be pope someday!

Swiezawski felt compelled to share this news with the cardinal. After Mass he found Wojtyla alone in the sacristy, putting away his vestments. The professor spoke plainly and with faith: "You will become Pope."

Again, other priests might have laughed or, worse, puffed out their chests at the very idea. The cardinal did neither. He didn't even reply with words. He simply looked deeply into the eyes of his friend and then walked away in profound thought.[6]

And then came the day before the actual conclave to choose Pope Paul's successor, when another old friend of Wojtyla gave voice to a prophecy—or perhaps it was more of a wish.

Father Mieczyslaw Maliński was concelebrating Mass with Cardinal Wojtyla when a nun read aloud the Prayers of the Faithful, the petitions being asked of God on behalf of the people. When she finished Father Maliński added this prayer: "We beseech thee, O Lord, by the intercession of St Bartholomew, whose feast we are celebrating, to bring it about that Cardinal Wojtyla is elected Pope."

There was a pause before the congregation gave the response: "Lord, graciously hear us."

Father Maliński nervously peeked at the cardinal. Wojtyla clasped his hands and held them to his mouth, deep in prayer. It was time for Karol to begin the Offertory, yet he did not make a move or a sound.

The rector decided to add another petition. "For holiday-makers in Italy," he suggested weakly.

"Lord, graciously hear us," the people chorused again.

Finally Cardinal Wojtyla added his own carefully worded petition: "We beseech thee, almighty God, that if a man is chosen as Pope who does not believe himself capable of bearing the heavy responsibility of being the vicar of thy Son, thou wilt give him the courage to say as St Peter did: 'Depart from me, for I am a sinful man, O Lord.' But if he should accept the burden, we beg thee to grant him enough faith, hope and love to bear the cross thou layest upon him."

To that humble prayer the congregation once more replied, "Lord, graciously hear us!" That was the end of the petitions.[7]

God heard both Maliński's and Wojtyla's prayers, though the successor to the throne of Peter would not be Cardinal Wojtyla yet.

### HELLO, GOOD-BYE

There were two cardinals who were considered front-runners in the election: Giovanni Benelli of Florence and Giuseppe Siri of Genoa. Both were, of course, Italian.

Some voters treated the secret election process as though it were a political instead of a spiritual event. They gossiped, divided into "camps" and tried to promote their choices for pope. Apparently this was not the will of the Holy Spirit, however, and plans to have either favorite elected backfired. A quiet man, Albino Luciani of Venice, was elected pope, and in honor of the two men who had served before him, he took the name John Paul I.

An exceedingly humble man, Pope John Paul I refused to be crowned with the papal tiara at the traditional "incorona-tion" ceremony. He instead accepted the tall bishop's hat, the mitre. He wanted to express the fact that Christ is King, and the pope is a shepherd who serves under him.[8]

John Paul I felt so unworthy of the position he now found himself in that his first words to the voting cardinals were, "May God forgive you for what you have done!"[9] He was no Vatican insider either. When it came time for his first meal as pope, he had no idea where the dining room was. He turned to Cardinal König of Vienna and asked, "Where do I go for dinner?"[10]

In his first official address, the new pope announced to the crowd that he had neither the wisdom of John XXIII nor the intelligence of Paul VI. The people responded with warmth and acceptance. But neither his promising leadership nor the support of the people had the chance to develop. Shockingly, just thirty-three days after his election, John Paul I died of a massive heart attack. All the voting cardinals were called to another conclave.

It was a conclave that Cardinal Wojtyla almost missed. The death of Pope John Paul I had shaken him, and perhaps he felt the heavy breath of destiny on the back of his neck. The weekend before the conclave was to start, he went off to pray at the Mountain Shrine of Mary at Mentorella. In the quiet of the mountains he was able to pray for guidance. Before heading back to the Vatican, he chatted with a Polish monk he encountered there. Finally, with only a few hours to spare, he set off to catch the bus back to Rome.

It was a two-mile trek down a valley to the bus station. He arrived on time, but the bus broke down thirty miles from its destination. The cardinal told a villager that he desperately needed to get to the conclave before the doors were locked. This man directed him to a local bus driver, who happened to be on vacation. The driver decided that the cardinal's situation was an important enough reason to put his holiday on hold, and he started up his bus.

## ONE GOOD SHOT

Wojtyla's arrival in Rome garnered little attention. According to the Italian media, Cardinal Siri and Cardinal Benelli were again considered the top two papabili. Eager to get interviews and pictures of them—as well as the other voting cardinals—over a thousand reporters from all over the globe had gathered in St. Peter's Square. Journalists from England, France, Spain, Portugal and the United States made up the majority, but there was one man representing India, Professor George Menachery.

The professor was an avid follower and student of papal elections. Eager to soak up the excitement and see history in the making, he had decided to fly to Rome and work as a freelance reporter on the event. He was fortunate enough to win by lot one of fourteen special passes that allowed him to be stationed right at the doors of St. Peter's Basilica. There one could take the best pictures of the cardinals as they arrived for the election Mass. And there Menachery waited.

When Benelli and Siri appeared, each surrounded by admirers, photographers jostled one another for the best shots. If one of these two were to become pope, the right photograph could be worth an enormous amount of money. Professor Menachery was no paparazzo, and he took only one photograph of each man.

No one seemed interested in taking a photograph of the "solitary figure in red approaching from the huge gateway." To Menachery this cardinal "looked lonely, tired and crestfallen, yet somehow upholding the dignity of a prince of the Church." Menachery also noted: "He alone among all the Cardinals arrived on foot, walking hurriedly towards the

Basilica.... [H]e was without benefit of admirers and supporters. One or two of the big-time photographers from the US were looking at this pitiable figure almost it seemed contemptuously."

Realizing that he still had a few shots left in his camera, Menachery thought to himself, "Why not snap him, whom nobody appears to care for?" He took a picture of the "lonely man," knowing neither his name nor his country. A surprised Cardinal Wojtyla raised his head and proceeded into the basilica without a word.

Later the professor would purchase from a besieged newsboy a copy of a picture of the new pope supplied by *L'Osservatore Romano*. He was surprised to see the familiar face of "the lonely hero of my photograph keenly looking at me from the front page."[11]

## HEARING THE CALL

The cardinals met in the Sistine Chapel, where they concelebrated the Holy Mass. They sang again, "*Veni, Creator Spiritus*," a plea for the Holy Spirit to be among them.

Then each cardinal moved to the desk and chair provided him on one of the two platforms that ran down the length of the chapel. The two rows of cardinals faced one another, and on every desk was a special pad and pencil, exactly the same for everyone in order to preserve anonymity. With these they would write down the surname of the person whom they wanted to be pope. After all the votes had been collected into an urn, three cardinals would count them and read them aloud, as three other cardinals would check their work for errors. The rules were clear: In order to become pope, a candidate had to receive two-thirds of the votes plus one.

On the first vote, as in the previous conclave, neither Benelli nor Siri were able to garner enough votes. The ballots were then burned with hay and an additive to blacken the smoke that escaped from the chimney. This was to signal those who waited outside—and the world who watched on television—that no pope had been elected yet. Then the cardinals turned in for the night. They would be sequestered until the new pope was elected.

At one point between that night and the next day, Cardinal Maximilian De Fürstenberg approached Wojtyla and stated as a question: "God is here, and calling you?"[12]

The following day, after a second round of voting, the ballots were carefully counted, and the same name was heard again and again: "Wojtyla...Wojtyla...Wojtyla..." Cardinal Wojtyla's face grew redder and redder as he listened. Finally he placed his head in his hands.

When it became clear that the necessary number of votes had been reached—and surpassed—the room exploded in applause. However, a man is not officially pope until he has replied to the question from the dean of the College of Cardinals: "Do you accept your canonical election as Supreme Pontiff?" with the answer, "*Accepto.*" Wojtyla's response was a bit longer, and his last words as a cardinal were, "With obedience in faith to Christ, my Lord, and with trust in the Mother of Christ and the church, in spite of great difficulties, I accept."[13]

Then he was asked what name he wished to take. In homage to his predecessor, he replied, "John Paul II."

The ballots were burned again, only this time the smoke was white. As the Vatican bells began tolling, people throughout the city of Rome turned to one another and exclaimed, "It's white! It's white! We have a new pope!" Thousands of Italians, tourists and media people began running to St. Peter's Square to join the thousands who already were waiting there.

## AT HOME IN ROME

As the dark night sky arched over the dome of St. Peter's, the balcony on which the new pope was to be revealed was alight with the help of electronics and—probably even more so—excitement. Finally the moment came for the announcement. Cardinal Pericle Felici, the senior cardinal-deacon, stepped up to the microphone and said the words everyone was waiting to hear: "*Habemus Papam!* (We have a pope!)"

The crowd roared their approval. Continuing in Latin, Cardinal Felici introduced the new pontiff: "*Carolum Sanctae Romanae Ecclesiae Cardinalem Wojtyla,*" who would be taking the name "*Ioannem Paulum Secundum.*"[14]

The crowd cheered again, although many did not know who *Carolum Cardinalem Wojtyla* was. It was obvious that the new bishop of Rome wasn't Italian.

The people were happy to know that the Church had a new shepherd, and the excitement was contagious. The crowds became even more excited when the pope, waving and smiling, stepped forward and spoke, something that a pope rarely did upon his introduction. He greeted the crowd in Italian: "Praised be Jesus Christ!"

The crowd cheered, delighted at hearing their language from an obvious foreigner. He continued: "Dear Brothers and Sisters…now the eminent cardinals have called a new bishop of Rome. They have called him from a far country: far, but always near through the communion of faith and in the Christian tradition.... I was afraid to receive this nomination, but I did it in the spirit of obedience to our Lord Jesus Christ and in total confidence in his Mother, the most holy Madonna." Between each carefully enunciated sentence, the crowd cheered with approval.

He smiled down at the people, and leaning on the balcony as though he were having an intimate conversation with one person, he continued, "I don't know if I can make myself clear in your...*our* Italian language...." The crowd went wild. He continued, "If I make a mistake"—and the crowd immediately protested, "Nooooo!"—"you will correct me." Only the Italian was more like, "You will me correct." The mistake didn't matter, for the people were thoroughly charmed and on his side.

"And so," the new pope concluded, "I present myself to you all, to confess our common faith, our hope, our trust in the Mother of Christ and of the Church, and also to start anew on this road of history and the Church, with the help of God and with the help of men."[15]

### The News Hits Poland

Poland, it turned out, would be the last to get the news, as the Communist government controlled all means of communication. Hours after the announcement in St. Peter's Square, the news made it to Polish radio: A *Pole* was now *pope!*

Bells pealed from nearly every tower and belfry, calling people together to hear the news. The Polish public went wild with elation. Spontaneous celebrations broke out everywhere, as people flooded the streets, waving Polish flags and weeping with ecstatic disbelief. Strangers embraced each other. Tributes of floral bouquets began piling up in front of the cardinal's former residence.

Ringing the bells of the local church in Wadowice, the town of Karol's birth, was his old friend and former catechism teacher, Father Edward Zacher. He had been overjoyed to hear the news that Lolek—*their* Lolek—was pope, and he was bursting to let the town know. The townspeople quickly gathered, filling the church to standing-room-only status, and demanded to know what all the fuss was about. When Father Zacher opened his mouth to tell them, he was too moved to speak, and one of his assistants stepped forward with the news.[16]

Not everyone in Poland was thrilled, however. Marek Sotek, a little boy of four and a half, could not understand the glee of his fellow countrymen. He didn't know what a pope was. What he *did* know was that the news of this John Paul II character had taken over Polish television, and the children's shows he had wanted to watch that evening were cancelled. All around him people were "happy and crying," but he hardly saw a reason to celebrate. In fact, "I hated him," Sotek now admits with some amusement.

Things went from bad to worse for poor little Marek. On Sunday John Paul II was scheduled to celebrate his first papal Mass, an event that was more than enough cause to preempt all regularly scheduled programming—including again the usual children's shows. Seething, Marek let his parents know just what he thought about the whole situation, and "I even said a few bad words."

His parents punished him, but on top of that he had to deal with a whole month of Sundays without his favorite shows. "Poland cancelled regular Sunday television for a month" in order to provide more coverage of the new pope, the now *Father* Marek told this author. So while he would later grow to be a great admirer of John Paul II, in the beginning, Sotek remembers, "I didn't like the pope *at all*."[17]

## BROTHER IN THE LORD

At the celebratory meal with the cardinals, Pope John Paul II did not sit down at the head table and wait to be served, as was expected of a new pope. Rather he popped open a bottle of champagne and proceeded to fill glasses—including those of the nuns who had prepared the meal. The fact that he was the first Pole to become pope was never far from his mind. He belted out Polish folk songs with Cardinal Stefan Wyszyński and Philadelphia's Cardinal John Krol, who was also of Polish descent.[18]

At the papal investiture Mass on October 22, Wojtyla sat robed in gold, and the cardinals lined up to honor him. One by one they knelt before him to kiss the Fisherman's Ring, which identified him as the successor of Saint Peter. The pope then kissed each man in return.

But when Cardinal Wyszyński knelt before him, John Paul II was filled with emotion. Some believed the orphaned pope shared a father-son relationship with the elder cardinal; others saw them as rivals. But at that moment the men were brothers. Wrapping an arm around the cardinal, John Paul humbly pressed his face against Wyszyński's head and kissed his hand, a scene that all present found meaningful.

Cardinal Wyszyński also made an interesting prophecy when he told the new pope that God has chosen him to lead the Church into the new millennium.[19] After having two popes die in one year, it must have been the Holy Spirit who inspired such a prediction. The new millennium was a quarter-century away.

From the beginning of his papacy, the Polish pope wanted to make it clear that he was a pope for all people and all nations. In his first homily, which was broadcast on radio and television all around the world, he expressed greetings in Italian, Polish, English, French, German, Spanish, Portuguese, Czechoslovakian, Russian, Ukranian and Lithuanian. He said: "...Today a new Bishop comes to the Chair of Peter in Rome, a Bishop full of trepidation, conscious of his unworthiness. And how could one not tremble before the greatness of this call and before the universal mission of this See of Rome!"

This trepidation was not fear, however. It was humility; it was awe of God. For the power of the Lord, the pope said, was "absolute" yet also "sweet and gentle." "It does not speak the language of force," he said, "but expresses itself in charity and truth."

He went on to urge, "Brothers and sisters, do not be afraid to welcome Christ and accept his power. Help the Pope and all those who wish to serve Christ and with Christ's power to serve the human person and the whole of mankind. Do not be afraid. Open wide the doors for Christ. To his saving power open the boundaries of States, economic and political systems, the vast fields of culture, civilization and development. Do not be afraid!"[20]

Pope John Paul II would become the most traveled pope in the history of the Catholic Church. One of his first trips was a quick one back to Mentorella, at the Marian shrine where he had been praying before the conclave. The cardinal who had left in a rickety old bus returned by papal helicopter.

Word quickly spread that the pope had arrived, and soon there was a great crowd gathered on the mountain. Two weeks earlier he had been able to pray there anonymously, and now he was sorry for the inconvenience this visit caused the Resurrectionist Fathers who ran the shrine. However, he felt it was his duty to return because "prayer... [is] the first task and almost the first signal of the Pope, just as it is the first condition of his service in the Church and in the world."[21]

## ❧ 5 ❧

## A New Kind of Pope

"THIS IS NOT A POPE FROM POLAND," FRENCH JOURNALIST André Frossard wrote after the election of John Paul II, "this is a Pope from Galilee."[1]

From the beginning, his smiling, approachable presence literally drew people to John Paul II. This was proven during his first Christmas season as pope, when he stopped to admire the Nativity scene that had been set up near the Vatican by the street cleaners of Rome. The daughter of one of the cleaners stepped forward and asked the Holy Father if he would officiate at her wedding. She didn't know that popes usually don't celebrate weddings, as the demand would be overwhelming and intrude on all of their other obligations. But the new pope agreed, and he joined Vittoria Janni and Mario Maltese in the holy sacrament of matrimony on February 25, 1979.

John Paul II was so popular that sometimes his admirers came to his front door—or his apartment window. The day after his first Christmas as pope, a crowd gathered beneath his window at St. Peter's, despite there being no general audience or prayer scheduled for that day. The crowd numbered in the hundreds, and they continued to clap and call for the pope until noon, when he appeared at the window and prayed the Angelus with them.

People would talk about the palpable energy and love that charged the air whenever the pope interacted with people of goodwill. And it was to such people that he addressed his first encyclical.

## THE TRIUMPH OF THE CROSS

Encyclicals are letters written by the pope, usually to the bishops of the world, that are often used to correct or clarify a Church teaching. However, John Paul's first encyclical, released in March of 1979, was addressed to the whole Church and to every man and woman of goodwill. Instead of delivering a message that was meant to fix a problem, it was more positive in tone, reminding everyone of the dignity of the human person thanks to the Incarnation of Jesus Christ. The life, death and resurrection of Jesus, the pope said, returned to man that value, greatness and dignity that was his at the Creation.

Called *Redemptor Hominis* ("The Redeemer of Man"), the encyclical went on to say that because of this dignity, the human person has certain inalienable rights, including the right to the freedom of religion. To deny man his right to worship God is to deny him his dignity and his freedom to serve his fellow man in truth and love.[2]

The message of this encyclical, although addressed to the entire world, held particular meaning for the people in Poland and their political situation. Still under Communist oppression, religious freedom was a privilege of the past and a fantasy of the future. Despite this, Pope John Paul II wanted to visit Poland and bring the hope and triumph of the cross to his homeland.

No pope had ever come from Poland, and no pope had ever visited there. The Polish people were filled with excitement at the very idea that their native son should return as the head of the Catholic Church. The Communists were not. They didn't want the Polish pope to come and steer the people back to religion and possibly to revolt. So the government simply refrained from inviting him.

Not to be deterred, the pope invited himself. He sent an official letter expressing his readiness to come to Poland whenever the country was ready to receive him. This letter prompted much arguing among the men in power. Some in the regime thought that proving themselves diplomatic hosts by giving John Paul a welcome worthy of a "national" would put them in a good political light. Others felt that a man of God deserved no welcome at all.

Leonid Brezhnev, the leader of the Soviet Communist Party, said that, since the pope was a "wise man," why not suggest that he bow out gracefully by claiming to be sick?[3]

The pope was not one to be controlled. Nevertheless, the Communist Party continued to try to manipulate his unavoidable visit to their best advantage. In an anticipatory strike, they dispatched a set of written instructions to the teachers of Poland in order to "intensely develop" all efforts to "atheize the youth." The pope was their enemy, the instructions said, and "[d]ue to his uncommon skills and great sense of humor he is dangerous, because he charms everyone."[4]

The pope's first choice of dates included the feast day of Saint Stanislaw, the patron of Poland, on May 8. Not wanting the pope to get his way completely—let alone arrive on the heels of May Day—government officials offered him nine days in June instead. Wanting to appear generous, they expanded his visit by seven days.

In doing this the officials unknowingly scheduled the pope's first public Mass in Poland for the Eve of Pentecost, the birthday of the Church! The Scriptures tell us that on Pentecost the Holy Spirit rushed down upon the apostles, filling them with the power and courage to stand up against their oppressors and spread the Good News. Pope John Paul II could not have been more satisfied with this turn of events.

## HOMECOMING

The pilgrimage began in Warsaw. When the pope arrived in his beloved homeland, he kissed the ground, as was his custom in all his travels. The gesture was packed with more personal meaning than usual.

After acknowledging and thanking the leaders who had made his visit possible, he turned to the people, who were waving flags of red and white (the Polish flag) or yellow and white (the papal colors). He shouted his triumphant greeting, "Praised be Jesus Christ!" Thunderous cheers came in reply.[5]

Hundreds of thousands of people lined the streets and tossed flowers at the pope as his motorcade passed by. He stopped at Victory Square to say Mass. A giant cross draped with a priestly stole stood behind him as he offered up Christ in the Eucharist.

While at first the Communist leaders did not want to televise the event, they eventually decided to do so in hopes that citizens wouldn't feel the need to witness any of it in person. The broadcast was carefully edited to tone down the excitement of the visit and excluded any actual shots of the pope!

The government ploy failed miserably. An estimated one million Poles filled the streets to attend one Mass. In his homily that day, John Paul II told the crowd that the suffering their country had undergone—particularly in recent history—showed that God had chosen them to be special witnesses to Christ. Then he asked the people if they were ready to live up to that responsibility. Their reply was a cry of deepest hunger: "We want God! We want God! We want God!"[6]

By the end of day one, the Communists knew that they were in trouble. The pope moved on to Gniezno and Czestochowa, where he made an emotional visit to Jasna Góra and prayed at the shrine of the Black Madonna.

In Kraków the pope acknowledged many familiar faces from his motorcade, calling people by name and waving as he passed by. He gently chided those who tried to grab his cassock as though he were a rock star. He stayed for three nights at his former residence at Franciszkańska, 3, and every evening a crowd gathered outside his window and serenaded him. Standing on the windowsill so that the people could get a better view of him, he sometimes sang along. By midnight he would have to ask the crowd for silence so that he could get some sleep.

On June 10, his last day in Kraków, he celebrated a Mass in Blonie Field. Despite every effort by the Communists to make sure that the Mass was not publicized in any way, the crowd was estimated at two to three times the numbers in Warsaw. John Paul II did not waste this opportunity to preach to literally millions of people. He extended his hands over the crowd in "that apostolic gesture" and called down a Polish Pentecost from heaven:

> I speak for Christ himself: "Receive the Holy Spirit!"
>
> I speak too for St. Paul: "Do not quench the Spirit!"
>
> I speak again for St. Paul: "Do not grieve the Spirit of God!"
>
> You must be strong, my brothers and sisters! You must be strong with the strength that faith gives! You must be strong with the strength of faith! You must be faithful! You need this strength today more than [in] any other period of our history....
>
> You must be strong with love, which is stronger than death. When we are strong with the Spirit of God, we are also strong with the faith of man.... There is therefore no need to fear.... Never lose your trust, do not be defeated, do not be discouraged....Always seek spiritual power from Him from whom countless generations of our fathers and mothers have found it. Never detach yourselves from Him. Never lose your spiritual freedom.[7]

### STO LAT!

The youth of Poland turned out in the tens of thousands to hear the pope speak outside of St. Michael's Church at Skalka. They serenaded him with every kind of instrument and chanted the traditional Polish blessing *Sto lat* ("May you live for a hundred years")! They then chanted, "Stay with us!"[8] which moved John Paul II very deeply. He had not been in Poland in months, and he did not know when he would be able to return again.

Just when the pope thought the young people couldn't affect him any more, they silently lifted a twelve-foot cross from somewhere in the crowd. This was followed by a garden of thousands of smaller crosses, which the youth removed from hiding inside coats and shirts and held high. The people from whom God had been kept, the people who wanted God, even the youngest people who only knew life under Communism—all had God. He lived in their hearts.

As his limousine drove away that evening, John Paul buried his face in his hands and cried. He cried that he had to leave his beloved homeland again, but his tears were also tears of gratitude and hope. Poland would prevail. God had shown this by raising up a man from among them to be their spiritual leader. John Paul knew that he would not leave his people orphans. He knew that the Holy Spirit remained behind to do the work of God.

The pope's message "Do not be afraid!" was one that the Polish people heard in their hearts. They heard him as a people, as a community and as individuals. His message would go on to echo within each of them and help see them through the remaining years of their struggle against Communist rule and beyond. They would remember what the pope did for them with gratitude.

"During communism, we were all very scared. But when he spoke, he empowered us," Barbara Dzidowska, a Polish woman who later moved to the United States, remembered in an interview with *New York Post* reporter Lorena Mongelli. "He gave me the strength to go on and to appreciate life."

Artist Karol Partyka, another Polish emigré, echoed the message. "The most important thing... the pope told us [was] not to be afraid... even if you have problems." Partyka was only twenty-one when the pope visited Kraków. Even twenty-five years later he could vividly remember the elder Karol's taking his hands and telling him, "Never give up."

Partyka, filled with emotion, could only reply, "Thank you, thank you," over and over. He would later bring visual expression to this gratitude by making a life-sized bronze sculpture of the pope, which now stands in front of St. Stanislaus Kostka Church in Greenpoint, Brooklyn.[9]

John Paul's prayerful and peaceful visit to Poland accomplished what no demonstration or protest could: It created a crack in the dam that was Poland's Communist government. He made waves in the river of freedom, which now surged against the wall of that dam. Over the next year the crack became bigger and bigger, as Communism's hold on Poland began to erode.

Lech Walesa, an unemployed electrician, saw that crack. He led a group made up of a wide range of Polish citizens in an anti-Communist social movement called "Solidarity." Using nonviolence as their "weapon," they were able to build an independent, self-governing trade union and get it legally recognized by the Communist government.

Within ten years Communism would die with a whimper

in Poland. Despite all of Walesa's work, he knew that the credit was not his. When the Communist government had legally recognized Solidarity, Walesa had signed the agreement with a giant pen commemorating the pope's visit to Poland. Topping that pen was a picture of John Paul's smiling face.

## SAINTS OF OUR TIME

Flowers from a throng of admirers rained on the pope's car as it entered the gates of the Auschwitz concentration camp. The bright, cheerful blooms and the pope's white cassock and long red cape contrasted with the grayness that was Poland's most notorious Nazi death camp.

Slowly Pope John Paul II walked into the courtyard of the camp, crunching through the sharp stones of the gravel path. In a row of barracks made of dull red brick, he stopped at Block 11. There he descended into the basement to visit Cell 18, a windowless, dank pit where Maximilian Kolbe, a Catholic priest, had died a slow and agonizing death.

A quiet Franciscan friar, Father Kolbe had managed to help shelter two thousand Jews from the Nazis before being arrested by the SS in 1941. When a fellow prisoner escaped from the camp, the Nazis decided to deter any other attempts by selecting ten men from his barracks to die in his stead. When one of the prisoners chosen to die protested because he had a wife and children, Father Kolbe stepped forward and offered to take his place. The Nazis accepted his offer, and they threw him into the pit with the other nine, leaving them to starve.

Death was more than three weeks in coming. All the while, Father Kolbe led his fellow prisoners in prayer and song. When only he and three others remained alive, the Nazis finished them off by lethal injection.

Pope John Paul II stood in the doorway of Cell 18, his head bowed in prayer. He deeply admired Kolbe because he had sacrificed his life for another and had shown others how to die.

Kolbe also had shown those who witnessed his sacrifice how to live. Although the prisoner who escaped was recaptured and drowned in the camp latrine, the man whom Kolbe saved, Franciszek Gajowniczek, survived to see his family again. In fact, he was at Auschwitz to embrace the pope when he visited in 1979. And he stood in St. Peter's Square with his wife and grandchildren when John Paul II declared Kolbe a saint on October 10, 1982.

Pope John Paul II would canonize more than 460 saints and declare over 1,250 men and women "blessed." That's more than any other pope before him. Many of them, like Maximilian Kolbe, had lived and died in John Paul's lifetime.

Edith Stein, whom the pope canonized on October 11, 1998, also died the holy death of a martyr at the hands of the Nazis. The youngest child of a large Jewish family, she had given up prayer and her belief in God in her early teens. Like the pope, she studied phenomenology and the works of Max Scheler.

Her studies in philosophy drew her back to God. After staying up all night to read the autobiography of Saint Teresa of Avila, she put the book down with the words, "This is the truth."[10]

Edith converted to Catholicism and became a Carmelite nun known as Saint Teresa Benedicta of the Cross. As the

Nazis took over Germany, Edith realized that "God had laid his hand heavily on His people and that the destiny of these people would also be mine."[11] Yet she welcomed that future, saying, "Human activities cannot help us...only the suffering of Christ. It is my desire to share in it."[12]

She prepared herself for this destiny by prayer, which led her to contemplate Queen Esther of the Old Testament, "who was taken away from her people precisely because God wanted her to plead with the king on behalf of her nation."[13] She wrote in her will, "I joyfully accept in advance the death God has appointed for me, in perfect submission to his most holy will. May the Lord accept my life and death...for the Jewish people, that the Lord may be received by his own and his Kingdom come in glory, for the deliverance of Germany and peace throughout the world...."[14]

Edith's sister Rosa had also converted and was working in the convent when the Nazis arrived. Taking her sister by the hand, Edith marched unafraid toward death, saying, "Come, Rosa. We're going for our people."[15] The two were forced into a train bound for Auschwitz on August 7, 1942. Two days later they died in the gas chamber.

Pope John Paul II addressed particularly the young people who gathered for the canonization of Edith Stein. "Your life is not an endless series of open doors," he said. "Listen to your heart! Do not stay on the surface but go to the heart of things! And when the time is right, have the courage to decide! The Lord is waiting for you to put your freedom in his good hands."[16]

## The Mercy Pope

Another saint who offered up her life for God's people, though she was not a martyr in the literal sense, was Helena Kowalska, better known as Saint Faustina. When Pope John Paul II canonized her on April 30, 2000, he claimed that it was the happiest day of his life.

In order to understand why, we would have to go back seventy-four years to April of 1926. While little Lolek was "growing in wisdom and strength" in Wadowice, a young novice in Kraków was accepting her habit in the convent of the Congregation of the Sisters of Our Lady of Mercy. Helena Kowalska took the name Sister Mary Faustina of the Most Blessed Sacrament.

By 1931 Karol Wojtyla was also in Kraków. At this time Sister Faustina, who was by all accounts a simple and humble woman, began receiving startling visions of Jesus Christ as "the King of Mercy." In these visions the Lord stood before her dressed in white, with one hand touching his heart and the other held aloft in blessing. Two rays emanated from his chest, one the color of blood, the other one light and somewhat transparent in appearance.

Jesus commanded the nun to commission a painting of this image and to have the words *Jezu, ufam tobie!* that is, "Jesus, I trust in you!" painted below it. She was to have the picture reproduced and distributed around the world. Thus, Jesus told her, she would perpetuate the kingdom of God by spreading his message of immense loving kindness and infinite mercy. He also requested that the image "be solemnly blessed on the first Sunday after Easter; that Sunday is to be the Feast of Mercy."[17]

When Sister Faustina came forward with this news, no one believed her, and the poor nun suffered only ridicule, accusation and judgment. But Jesus persisted in his call to her, and she remained faithful and obedient throughout her trials. Eventually two priests were won over to her mission.

The image was finally painted in 1934 by Eugene Kazimierowski. By the next year, during the celebration of the Jubilee Year of the Redemption of the World, it was displayed publicly at the Eastern Gate to Vilnius, Poland, on the Sunday after Easter. Thousands of people came to venerate it, and devotion to the Divine Mercy quickly spread.

Appealing to God's mercy would become more and more important, Jesus warned Faustina, because a terrible war was soon coming upon the world, and Poland was in grave danger. The sister died of tuberculosis in 1938, a year before Poland fell to Nazi occupation. She left behind a compelling, nearly 700-page diary that recounted her relationship with Christ and his message of Divine Mercy.

The message of Divine Mercy spread during the war, particularly in Poland. Pilgrims from throughout the country came to the congregation's chapel and Faustina's tomb to plead for her intercession and to ask the Lord God, "For the sake of his sorrowful passion, have mercy on us and on the whole world."

The Divine Mercy devotion continued to spread around the world until 1959, when badly translated and mistaken versions of the devotion came to the attention of the Holy See, which banned it. However, Sister Faustina and her devotion found an ally in the bishop of Kraków, Karol Wojtyla. He personally worked to obtain the documentation needed to validate and reinstate the devotion. His tireless efforts paid off when the Church lifted the ban in 1978, twenty years after it had been imposed.

By then Karol was Cardinal Wojtyla, and within six months he would be elected Pope John Paul II. He would take the theme of God's mercy as the subject of his second encyclical, *Dives in Misericordia* ("The Mercy of God"). He wrote, "Jesus Christ taught that man not only receives and experiences the mercy of God, but that he is also called 'to practice mercy' towards others."[18]

The themes of Divine Mercy and of the dignity of life ran throughout John Paul II's papacy like the parallel rails of a train track. He not only canonized Sister Faustina Kowalska but also, to the surprise of many, established Divine Mercy Sunday as a feast day for the entire Church. The feast is on the First Sunday after Easter, just as Jesus had told the saint it should be.

## THE GREAT ESCAPE

Although he thrived in his papal duties, Pope John Paul II sometimes missed the freedom to enjoy life's simple pleasures, such as being able to go skiing without any fanfare. So one day, in the winter of 1981, while staying in the papal villa in Castel Gandolfo, he planned a secret outing to the mountains.

For this venture he enlisted the help of two aides and his secretary. The group piled into a car belonging to one of the priests. The pope sat in the backseat, and one of the aides held a newspaper open to shield him from view as the car swept past security.

They continued on to Ovindoli, the central ski town. There they selected a quiet slope where the pope was able to ski privately all day long. When the day was over, a thrilled John Paul turned to his coconspirators and announced, "We did it!"

This covert skiing operation was repeated about a hundred times. Even when standing in line for the ski lift, the pope's "disguise" of a ski jacket, sunglasses and a beret usually allowed him to go unrecognized.

Once in a while, however, the pope's cover was blown. One time a ten-year-old boy came by the papal party. The boy had been cross-country skiing with his family but had straggled behind his group and lost sight of them. Seeing the pope's aides standing in a cluster, he stopped and asked if they had seen his family. As one of the priests directed him to his parents, the youthful, smiling Pope John Paul II finished his run down the mountainside with a spray of snow, right in front of the child.

The boy's mouth fell open. Then he began to point and yell frantically, "The pope! The pope!"

The priests hushed the child. They told him to stop being silly and go meet his family before he lost them again. Then the men dashed back to the car, bundled the pope inside and drove off before someone found out the child was right.[19]

## ❧ 6 ❧

## *"O Mary, My Mother!"*

POPE JOHN PAUL II'S FEARLESSNESS AROUND THOSE IN power and his message to those under oppression to "be not afraid" had the opposite effect on some people. And on May 13, 1981, someone—or some group—was scared enough of his success to try to silence the man and his message forever. Just before that fateful day, two tiny events seemed almost to prophesy—with irony—what was about to happen.

On May 6 the new contingent of the Swiss Guard presented themselves to the pope for his blessing. He said, "We pray to the Lord that violence and fanaticism may be kept far from the walls of the Vatican."[1]

And on May 12 the pope blessed the new Vatican ambulance with the words, "May it never be needed."[2]

### STRUCK DOWN
May 13 was the feast day of Our Lady of Fatima. In his devotion to the Blessed Mother, the pope was particularly fond of

feast days that honored her, and as crowds gathered in St. Peter's Square to attend his general audience, he joyfully went out to greet them.

It was 5:00 PM when his white papal Jeep began its circuit of the square. John Paul stood in the back, waving to the faithful as usual, sometimes stopping to reach out and shake hands with someone or to bless a child. One little girl, Sara Bartoli, held up a statue of Our Lady of Fatima, and John Paul took her in his arms and kissed the statue. He was handing the girl back to her parents when there was a strange popping sound. Confusion reigned as the pope fell backward into the arms of his faithful secretary, Monsignor Dziwisz. The pope had been shot.

"Where?" asked Monsignor Dziwisz.

"In the stomach," John Paul groaned.

"Does it hurt?"

"Yes. O Mary, my Mother! Mary, my Mother!"[3]

There was considerable damage to the pope's stomach and colon, causing him much pain. The photographs splashed across the front pages of the world's newspapers, however, showed an almost serene-looking John Paul II, a vision in white with blood covering his finger, which the bullet had grazed en route to his abdomen. Later the pope would state that despite his pain, he was comforted by the strong feeling that he would survive.

As his blood pressure plummeted, John Paul whispered prayers. He was quickly taken to the ambulance he had blessed the day before and then rushed to the hospital.

The would-be assassin, a twenty-three-year-old Turkish terrorist by the name of Mehmet Ali Agca, could not flee the scene as easily as he had hoped. Immediately after he fired his nine-millimeter pistol, he was seized by a Franciscan nun and subsequently tackled and wrestled to the ground by others in the crowd.[4]

The hospital was four miles away, but the ambulance made it there in record time—in less than twelve minutes. This was nothing short of miraculous, as the ride from the Vatican to the Agostino Gemelli University Polyclinic typically takes twenty-five to forty minutes, and the siren of the new ambulance wasn't working.

The person who did get stuck in traffic was the head surgeon, Dr. Francesco Crucitti. He was visiting a patient in another hospital across town when a distressed nun appeared at the doorway and announced that the pope had been shot. Bolting from the room, Dr. Crucitti asked for the nearest phone. After failing to contact anyone at Gemelli, he dashed for his car and was soon speeding down the city streets.

Then he found himself behind a line of cars that weren't moving. Seeing a convoy of police cars rocketing by in the other lane, Dr. Crucitti joined them, even though they were all going the wrong way on a two-way street. A policeman on a motorcycle sped up beside him, and Dr. Crucitti cried out, "I have to be at Gemelli immediately!"[5] The police escorted him the rest of the way.

Dr. Crucitti dashed into one of the waiting elevators open on the ground floor, ready to carry him to the ninth floor. The moment he stepped off the elevator, nurses surrounded him, tearing off his street clothes and replacing them with surgical scrubs. They informed him that the pope had lost consciousness and that his pulse was barely discernible.

Meanwhile, Monsignor Dziwisz administered the last rites, anointing the pope with holy oil and praying over him. Only then was John Paul II, the head of the Church and the monsignor's personal friend, ready for surgery.

Examining him, Dr. Crucitti made a terrible discovery: The pope's blood pressure was so dangerously low because he was bleeding internally—and profusely. Only a quarter of his blood supply was left in his veins. The doctor began operating immediately.

A steady flow of blood transfusions was pumped into the pope's body throughout the five-hour-and-twenty-minute surgery. Among the procedures that needed to be carried out before the pontiff could be transferred to the recovery room were sewing up the lacerations in his colon and removing over twenty inches of damaged intestine from his body.

Meanwhile, pilgrims remained in St. Peter's Square to offer up prayers on the pope's behalf. Others continued to stream in for the rest of the day, standing watch and tearfully awaiting some word on the pope's condition. People consoled one another, milling around the platform where the pope would have delivered his weekly message.

The sight of the pope's chair, seemingly abandoned and forlorn, prompted someone in the crowd to place an icon of the Black Madonna on it. After a while the picture fell over in a gust of wind, yet it continued to transmit its message. For written on the back of it was the legend: "May Our Lady protect the Holy Father from evil."[6]

The vigil was long. It was nearly one o'clock in the morning when it was announced that the surgery had been successful.

### A MOTHER PROTECTS HER SON

It was to Our Lady's prayers—and to the petitions of the faithful—that Pope John Paul credited his recovery. "One hand fired," he said from his hospital bed, "and another guided the bullet.... To you, Mary, I repeat: *Totus tuus ego sum*."[7]

Within days the pope was praying the Liturgy of the Hours daily and concelebrating Mass from his bed. His birthday was May 18, and he allowed his photograph to be taken and published. It showed him convalescent but sitting up and alert. The image provided comfort to Catholics around the world.

Prayers and wishes for a speedy recovery poured in from all over. Even Leonid Brezhnev sent a get-well message: "I am deeply indignant at the attempt on your life. I wish you a rapid and complete recovery."[8]

For days afterward the pope's suite of rooms on the tenth floor of the hospital served as a mini-Vatican, as he conducted his papal business from there. It was as he lay recuperating that he learned that Cardinal Wyszyński was dying. It took some wrangling to get the two men in touch by phone, but they were able to say good-bye before the cardinal's death on May 28.

Since it would be months before the pope would be well enough to greet the public again, he recorded messages to be broadcast over the sound system at St. Peter's Square. In his first message he announced that he was praying for the two American women who had been wounded by the same bullet that had injured him. "I am particularly close to [them]," he said, then he added, "I pray for that brother of ours who shot me, and whom I have sincerely pardoned. United with

Christ, Priest and Victim, I offer my sufferings for the Church and for the world."[9]

As soon as he had recovered sufficiently from his wounds, the pope would prove this forgiveness. In December he took time out from his busy schedule to stop at the Roman penitentiary where his would-be assassin was serving life in prison. He celebrated Mass, and afterward he sat down for an intimate twenty-minute conversation with Agca. When the men finished talking and rose from their chairs, Pope John Paul II held out his hand in an offer of forgiveness. Agca clasped it in acceptance, and the two men shook hands.

To this day it is not known publicly why Agca attacked the pope. Was he acting alone or in conjunction with some type of terrorist organization? Did he tell the pope during their private chat? To others Agca gave conflicting reasons for his action. He made so many outrageous claims—including that he was the Messiah—that one may safely assume that he was mentally unstable if not spiritually disturbed.

## THANKS TO OUR MOTHER

One year after the assassination attempt, it was again the feast day of Our Lady of Fatima, and Pope John Paul II made a pilgrimage to her shrine in Portugal. There, more than half a century before his visit, the Virgin Mary is said to have revealed herself to three shepherd children in a series of apparitions that covered more than six months. Although the children were very young and simple peasants (the oldest, Lucy, was only ten years old at the time), the Blessed Mother entrusted them with the responsibility of spreading her message to the world.

The message was not new, but it was insistent. Our Lady called for all people of the world to stop sinning, to make reparation for past sins, to offer up sacrifices to God and to pray always. She warned that if these instructions were not carried out, the world would call upon itself war and destruction. The children obediently carried out their assigned tasks, and the message of Fatima has been made known the world over.

After Pope John Paul II arrived at the shrine, he expressed his gratitude to Our Lady for protecting him:

> I come here today because on this very day last year in St. Peter's Square in Rome, the attempt on the Pope's life was made in mysterious coincidence with the anniversary of the first apparition at Fatima, which occurred on 13 May 1917.
>
> I seem to recognize in the coincidence of the dates a special call to come to this place. And so today I am here. I have come in order to thank divine providence in this place which the Mother of God seems to have chosen.
>
> Mary's motherhood…is manifested in a particular way in the places where she meets us: her dwelling places, places in which a special presence of the mother is felt…
>
> Mary's spiritual motherhood is therefore a sharing in the power of the Holy Spirit of "the giver of life"; it is the humble service of her who says of herself, "Behold, I am the handmaid of the Lord" [Lk 1:38].[10]

Two years later the bishop of Fatima, Alberto Amaral, visited Pope John Paul II in Rome and presented him with a statue of Our Lady of Fatima. The pope spent that very evening praying before it and giving thanks to God. Before Bishop Amaral departed for Portugal, the pope gave him a gift: the bullet that Dr. Crucitti had removed from his body on May 13, 1981.

"It doesn't belong to me," the pope told Amaral, "but to the One who took care of me and saved me. I want you to take it to Fatima…as a sign of my gratitude to the Most Blessed Virgin Mary and as a witness to the great deeds of God."

Amaral flew back to Portugal with the precious gift in a small black box. He presented it to the rector of Fatima, Father Luciano Guerra. For a while the two men wondered where in the sanctuary would be the best place to keep it. Then Bishop Amaral had an idea: "Do you think you could place the bullet in the crown of the statue?"

The crown on the statue of Our Lady of Fatima was made of hundreds of old pearls and thousands of other gemstones, including a large piece of turquoise to symbolize the planet Earth. The bullet would hardly enhance the ornamental beauty of the crown, and where could it be placed securely?

Then the rector saw the answer. The eight hoops that make up the main design of the crown meet at the base, forming a small hole. Father Guerra slipped the bullet inside. It was a perfect fit.[11]

## ❧ 7 ❧

### *Papal Encounters*

His solo performance for the pope was the defining moment of guitarist Tony Melendez's life.

It was September 15, 1987, in Los Angeles, California, and even though Melendez was a singer, music director, composer and musician, performing for the pontiff and an audience of thousands was daunting. He set aside his fears to play and sing a song aptly entitled "Never Be the Same."

When he was done, Tony didn't move; the security guards had told him not to. Instead it was John Paul who, after giving the young musician a standing ovation, started moving toward him. He walked the length of the stage and stopped briefly to look down at a woman in the audience below. Her back was turned to the pontiff to applaud Melendez, so the woman was surprised when John Paul suddenly placed his hand on her shoulder for balance and leapt off the four-foot platform into the audience.

The pope then walked up to the smaller stage and gestured for Tony to lean down. The pope took the musician's face in his hands and planted a kiss on one of his cheeks. The crowd cheered their approval. They were as impressed and inspired as the pope was by Mr. Melendez's performance. For Tony Melendez was born without arms; he had played the guitar with his feet.

"I felt like Jell-O, my body trembling from the emotion of it all," Tony remembers. After the encounter he blinked back tears of astonishment and gratitude, but he still managed to listen carefully as the pope gave him a special assignment.

"My wish for you, Tony, is to keep giving hope to all the people."

Tony took the words to heart. "Since [that day], I have been on and off the road, month by month, 10 venues, 20 to 25 days per month. His blessings continue through my singing."[1]

From the beginning of his papacy, John Paul II showed a special interest in the disabled. On his 1979 trip to the United States, he stopped at the Cathedral of the Holy Cross in Boston, where a vast number of priests and nuns had gathered to meet him. At the end of the visit, the pope was getting ready to head off for Boston Common, where he would celebrate Mass, when he spotted a young woman in a wheelchair.

Jane De Martino, twenty-six years old, had been paralyzed in an accident. John Paul took her hand, whispered some words of encouragement, gave her a kiss and left her with the gift of a gold-and-white rosary.

A policeman standing nearby watched the entire scene. He walked away weeping. "I've got to get back to the church," he said.[2]

## THE GOSPEL OF LIFE

"[I]n the name of God: respect, protect, love and serve life, every human life! Only in this direction will you find justice, development, true freedom, peace and happiness!"[3]

From the beginning of his priesthood, Pope John Paul II had held the dignity of the human person to be one of the hallmarks of his ministry. This idea took shape during World War II, when he witnessed the opposite attitude and the subsequent willful extermination of people who were deemed unworthy of life. Over the years he waged an ongoing fight to protect the lives of all people, from the unborn to the dying, of all races and creeds. In 1995 this effort became known as the "Gospel of Life" when he wrote an encyclical by that name.

"The Gospel of life," he wrote, "is at the heart of Jesus' message....The Gospel of God's love for man, the Gospel of the dignity of the person and the Gospel of life are a single and indivisible Gospel." He believed this because "[t]his saving event [of the Incarnation] reveals to humanity not only the boundless love of God who 'so loved the world that he gave his only Son' (Jn 3:16), but also the incomparable value of every human person."[4]

The Old Testament tells us that "God created man in his own image" (Genesis 1:27); the New Testament, that God came to earth in our image. The two defining moments in the history of the world delivered the same message: God, in his love of all people, made human life sacred. This was a philosophical truth for the pope. He wasn't making it up; he was simply pointing it out.

Unfortunately, the world didn't seem to want to accept this life-affirming message. "A new cultural climate [was] developing and taking hold."[5] John Paul called this attitude "the culture of death."[6] It was a new and even trendy spin on the eugenics efforts of the Nazis. "A person who, because of illness, handicap or, more simply, just by existing, compromises the well-being or life-style of those who are more favoured tends to be looked upon as an enemy to be resisted or eliminated," Pope John Paul wrote. This was a "conspiracy against life."[7]

The pope saw the disastrous and far-reaching effects of society's acceptance of this attitude:

[B]road sectors of public opinion justify certain crimes against life in the name of the rights of individual freedom, and on this basis they claim not only exemption from punishment but even authorization by the State, so that these things can be done with total freedom and indeed with the free assistance of health-care systems.

…Choices once unanimously considered criminal and rejected by the common moral sense are gradually becoming socially acceptable. Even certain sectors of the medical profession, which by its calling is directed to the defence and care of human life, are increasingly willing to carry out these acts against the person.[8]

The pope feared for life on earth. Despite the world's declaration after World War II, "Never again," the truth was that abortion, euthanasia and other forms of so-called health care were killing thousands of helpless people every day in "civilized" society. This was "tragic...grave and disturbing," the pope stated, and it was happening because the collective conscience of humanity had been "darkened" by "widespread conditioning," making it increasingly difficult for people "to distinguish between good and evil."[9]

Therefore, part of the Church's mission, Pope John Paul II wrote, is "the proclamation of the Gospel of life, an integral part of that Gospel which is Jesus Christ himself." Indeed, "[w]e are the people of life because God, in his unconditional love, has given us the Gospel of life and by this same Gospel we have been transformed and saved."[10]

## AIDS

In the 1980s the matter of life and death had a new name: AIDS. Acquired Immune Deficiency Syndrome surprised everyone when it suddenly became epidemic in many parts of the world.

Not much was known about the disease at the time, but there was certainly no cure, and there was widespread fear about how contagious the disease really was. In some places an AIDS patient could be run out of town or stoned. Even in the United States those with the disease suffered ostracism.

Through its schools, hospitals, hospices and charitable organizations, the Catholic Church was one of the first institutions to educate the public on the truth about AIDS and to provide care and compassion for those living with the disease. As an example to Catholics—and to all people—the pope reached out to those suffering from the disease. One photograph shows him warmly embracing a four-year-old boy living with AIDS.

The pope also made public statements to the effect that the disease was *not* God's condemnation upon sinners. "God loves you all, without distinction, without limit," he stated while on a visit to San Francisco in 1987. "He loves those of you who are sick, those suffering from AIDS.... He loves all with an unconditional and everlasting love."

While visiting AIDS patients in Tanzania, the pope emphasized the fact that the disease does not discriminate. "The drama of AIDS threatens...the whole of humanity. It knows no frontiers."

As a way to help stem the AIDS crisis, the pope called for abstinence outside of marriage and fidelity within it. In 2001 he proclaimed his solidarity with sufferers of the disease: "Dear brothers and sisters suffering from AIDS: Do not feel alone! The Pope is by your side and supports you with affection in your difficult path."[11]

## HEALING TOUCH

Pope John Paul II wanted people to know the God of love and healing, the God of infinite mercy. And for one family in Mexico, this was a lesson happily and gratefully learned.

Little Heron Badillo was only five years old, but he had already endured 500 spinal taps and been treated in five different hospitals. Skeletal and weak because of his inability to eat and bald from endless rounds of chemotherapy, he was fighting a losing battle with leukemia. Yet when his mother, Maria del Refugio Mireles Badillo, heard that the pope would be visiting Mexico, she had hope. With the desperate faith that maternal love produces, she believed that presenting her son to the pope would bring healing.

Maria decided that even though the trip would be arduous for her feeble son, they would be at the airport when the pope's plane landed. Her husband, on the other hand, disagreed. He was an atheist, and he simply didn't see the point in dragging their ailing son on a two-hour trip when they probably would only get to see the pope from a distance.

Refusing to be dissuaded, Maria drove Heron to the airport. There they found a place among the crowd where they could see the plane touch down. They watched eagerly as the pope, dressed all in white, disembarked. Their hearts sank when they realized that his designated route led away from them. Maria prayed that somehow the pope would ignore the route and walk in their direction instead. And he did.

Heron watched the shining gold cross that hung over the pope's heart grow larger as John Paul made his way toward him. Finally the boy looked up to see a face that beamed with joy. John Paul II laid his hand on Maria's shoulder and gestured for the mother and her son to release a dove they had brought with them. The pope then bent down, gently kissed Heron on top of his smooth, round head and walked away.

A grateful Maria returned to her car with her son. Once he was settled in, she heard words that were music to her ears. "Mom, I'm hungry.... I want some chicken."

Heron confessed to feeling something like "an electrical charge" when the pope touched him. Within months his leukemia disappeared. He stopped taking his medicine, his hair grew back, and he began to live a normal life. When Pope John Paul heard about the cure, he said simply, "God does great and miraculous things."

The Badillos believe that those great and wonderful

things were bona fide miracles—first that the pope approached them, and second that their son was healed of a fatal disease. Yes, all the Badillos believe this, because of a third miracle: Heron's physical healing brought with it a spiritual healing for his father, who became a devout Christian. In fact, Cardinal Javier Lozano Barragan once described the man's faith as greater than his own.[12]

# ❈ 8 ❈

## *Forever Young*

AN IMPORTANT PART OF THE LEGACY OF POPE JOHN PAUL II was his appeal to youth. He began the global phenomenon called World Youth Day in 1984. Wanting to mark the 1,950[th] anniversary of the death of Jesus Christ—and therefore the salvation of mankind—he proclaimed 1984 the Holy Year of Redemption. He arranged a variety of special events to take place around the world. One of these was to be an international youth gathering on Holy Thursday in Rome.

This "International Jubilee of Youth" drew more than three hundred thousand young people to St. Peter's Square. Despite its being the first event of its kind, everything went smoothly. Plans for a giant tent area to accommodate the pilgrims were cancelled, so 6,000 Roman families came forward to offer hospitality in their homes. The Stations of the Cross were conducted in the Coliseum, and Mass was celebrated at St. Peter's Basilica.

Given the success of this monumental gathering, a similar event was quickly arranged for the following year. Again hundreds of thousands of young people came to Rome in answer to the pope's call.

By Christmas of 1985, John Paul had decided that the Church should host a large-scale international youth gathering on a regular basis—preferably during Holy Week. Eventually the event was called World Youth Day, although it actually lasted four to five days. Arranged similarly to the Olympics, the gathering would be hosted by a selected country every two years, with a chosen motto and logo. During the alternate years Youth Days would be celebrated on the diocesan level, the first of these occurring in 1986.

The first international World Youth Day celebrated outside of Rome was in 1987 in Buenos Aires, Argentina. Santiago de Compostela, Spain, hosted the event in 1989. In 1991 it was brought to John Paul's beloved Czestochowa in Poland. The theme that year, "You Have Received a Spirit of Sonship" (Romans 8:15), was very much in keeping with the pope's spirituality.

Mary Ann Scales, from Franciscan University of Steubenville, was at Czestochowa in 1991. She recalls traveling with fellow students by bus from Holland to the Czech Republic and finally Poland. She met one of the bus drivers, a Dutchman and law student named Hedwyck, who made it clear that he was in no way a regular churchgoer. Yet his conversation proved him to be someone with a clear set of morals and faith in God. So by the time the group reached the Holy Mountain of Jasna Góra, he had decided to stick around and see what would happen.

The Holy Father, Mary Ann reports, "exuded such a presence of the Holy Spirit" that the group from Steubenville was overwhelmed with joy. And so, it seems, was their driver. He surprised the Steubenville students when he began gleefully "jumping up and down" at the sight of the pope.

The pope's arrival at a World Youth Day always created an impression. He didn't come with marching elephants, blaring trumpets or other fanfare. Rather there was a palpable energy that emanated from him and spread like electricity throughout the crowd. Participants in different World Youth Days report feeling what they describe as "energy" or "the Holy Spirit." They all agree on one word for their deepest feeling: love, the all-consuming yet peaceful presence of pure and utter love.

## DENVER, COLORADO, 1993

Before the pope arrived in the United States for World Youth Day 1993, the media's coverage anticipating the event was cynical. The event may have succeeded in other countries, they argued, but North American youth were a different breed of teenager altogether. How did the pope expect to reach them?

The prevailing opinion was that American teens were jaded consumers and therefore a tough sell. They were also multicultural and adventurous, not to mention used to doing what they wanted when they wanted. The press did not expect them to respond well to the head of a religious institution—especially an elderly Caucasian male from a foreign country who would tell them to sacrifice their desires, wait for gratification, give up material goods and follow God.

The media were sure that the pope would appear to be "out of touch" to modern youth.

The city of Denver had another problem that lowered media expectations. Record numbers of shootings had occurred within the three months prior to the event, creating a "summer of violence" in the area. Now the expected influx of thousands of extra people—in the blistering heat—did not bode well to some Denver inhabitants.

All the apprehensions proved unfounded. The rain preceding the pope's arrival stopped with Hollywood-like timing the moment the papal helicopter appeared. As it descended into Mile High Stadium in the midst of the Rocky Mountains, ninety thousand voices rose in the chant, "John Paul II! We love you! John Paul II! We love you!"

As the sun set behind the stadium, a rainbow arched over the audience. The Holy Father told the young people: "Jesus has called each one of you to Denver for a purpose: You must live these days in such a way that, when the time comes to return home, each one of you will have a clearer idea of what Christ expects of you."[1]

Eva Silva recalls John Paul's "holy aura," which brought her to tears. Only sixteen years old at the time, she had traveled to Denver with a youth group from the Bronx. Father Larry Paolicelli, who led the group to Colorado, noted that the students "had no idea that [the pope] would have this kind of effect on them. I think…the whole idea of concentrating on youth…[is] a beautiful vision, which has borne great fruit."[2]

The theme of this World Youth Day was from John 10:10: "I came that they might have life, and have it to the full." In his talks the pope warned the young people that the "culture of death" was "seek[ing] to impose itself on our desire to live and live to the full" by "reject[ing] the light of life" and "preferring the 'fruitless works of darkness.'" And the harvest of darkness was "injustice, discrimination, exploitation, deceit [and] violence."[3]

The pope pointed out that in the present century, like no other time in history, man has sought ways to legalize and justify atrocities against fellow human beings. In the name of freedom man has worked forcefully to remove the freedom of others through genocide, so-called ethnic cleansing and the taking of others' lives before birth and before natural death. Morality and goodness, the pope told the young people, are not subjective. They are the universal expectations of all people, who are all made in the image of God.

Young people appreciated the pope's speaking in this way to them. "We don't love the Pope because he's cute and cuddly, but because he tells us the truth!" exclaimed one.[4]

John Horsman, who was sixteen years old during the World Youth Day in Denver, believed that the pope addressed young people in this manner because "the pope cared for us."[5]

Peace reigned over the city of Denver throughout World Youth Day. Not a single crime was reported at the events, and peace would remain even after the crowds went home. The "summer of violence" had ended.

MANILA, 1995

"As the Father sent me, so am I sending you" (John 20:21). This was the theme of World Youth Day 1995, which occasioned the biggest gathering of people of all time. On January 14, 1995, four million youth came to Luneta Park in Manila for the pope's Mass. He did not let the opportunity go to waste. His homily challenged the youth to recognize the fact that God had commissioned them:

> Jesus says to you: "I am sending you to your families, to your parishes, to your movements and associations, to your countries, to ancient cultures and modern civilization, so that you will proclaim the dignity of every human being, … revealing to the world the true face of Jesus Christ, who is one with every man, every woman and every child, no matter how poor, no matter how weak or handicapped.
>
> How does Jesus send you? He promises neither sword, nor money, nor power, nor any of the things which the means of social communications make attractive to people today. He gives you instead grace and truth. He sends you out with the powerful message of his paschal mystery, with the truth of his cross and resurrection. That is all he gives you, and that is all you need.[6]

There were light-hearted moments at this World Youth Day too. It was obvious that the pope sincerely enjoyed being in the company of the young people and that they were taken with him. He enjoyed joking with the crowd and joining in their sing-alongs, sometimes standing shoulder-to-shoulder with the teenagers, holding their hands and swaying in time to the music.

At the start of the Saturday night vigil in Manila, the youth adopted the pope as one of their own, taking up the chant, "Lolek! Lolek!"

The pope smiled at the crowd. "Lolek is not serious," he told them. "But John Paul II is too serious." Then he reminded them, "[I]n the middle there was Karol."

Given this permission to address him by his Christian name, the crowd went wild. "Karol! Karol!" they shouted.[7]

The happy crowd did not know that a short eight days before, on February 6, a plot to assassinate the pope on their home soil had been foiled. Knowing that World Youth Day would attract a huge crowd, a group of terrorists had decided it would be an ideal event at which to make an "explosive" statement. They planned to detonate a bomb underneath the altar while the pope was celebrating Mass. Then, as the crowd stampeded in panic, snipers—perhaps dressed in cassocks they had stolen—would shoot into the crowd. It would be a tragedy of historic proportions.

Then came what perhaps can be described as divine intervention. One of the terrorists mistakenly set off the bomb on which he was working, starting a fire in the apartment where the group were staying. Once the fire was extinguished, police found evidence of the planned attack on the pope, including a computer disc containing a precise map of the route the popemobile was to take.

The lease on the apartment was traced to Wali Khan Amin Shah and Ramzi Ahmed Yousef. Yousef had been responsible for the 1993 attack on the World Trade Center. He was captured in Islamabad a month after the fire.

INNER STRENGTH

"Teacher, where are you staying?" "Come and see!" (see John 1:38–39). These words formed the theme of World Youth Day 1997 in Paris. Although the French media were as skeptical about the event as their counterparts in the United States had been, and even France's bishops had their doubts, it was as successful as its predecessors. No more than 250,000 people were expected to turn out, but twice that number teemed in the streets by day one of the festival. Parisians had never seen anything like it.

Even though the event was in August, the pope brought Holy Week to the city. Tuesday, the first day of the festival, represented Palm Sunday. The colossal World Youth Day cross was carried through the streets of Paris in a recreation of Jesus' triumphal entry into Jerusalem. Thursday became another Holy Thursday, with the pope reading from the Gospel about the washing of the feet. And on Friday the pope led everyone in praying the Stations of the Cross.

Much as in Denver, despite the record numbers of young people who attended the rally, there was not a single arrest made for the festival's duration. During those four days the safest place to be in Paris was at World Youth Day.

By 2002, when World Youth Day came to Toronto, Pope John Paul II was slowing down. His many physical ailments had ravaged his body to the point that even walking was a struggle. Yet whenever he was around young people, the pope seemed to draw energy from them. In his closest circle this phenomenon was referred to as the "youthening" of the pope.

Sister Mary Ann Walsh, a Sister of Mercy, witnessed this when the pope's plane landed at the Toronto airport. From the airplane window John Paul was able to see the great cheering crowd that had turned out to see him. His strength renewed at the sight, the pope surprised his entourage by choosing to walk down the steps instead of taking the lift that had been arranged to lower him from the plane.[8]

Shannon Federoff, who was in that crowd, said, "I was mesmerized by his face. When he first came in, he looked so tired, but...he seemed to feed off [the crowd's] enthusiasm. His face seemed a lot more animated suddenly."

As the event went on, Shannon saw the pope weaken. And even in his weakness he inspired her:

[He steadied himself] on the arms of his chair and [tried] to push himself up into a standing position.... He didn't want to stand so he could make himself more important; he tried to stand because he was thinking of all the people coming from afar to catch a glimpse of him. He pushed and pushed against the arms of the chair, but his body was just too weak to obey him. After raising himself a few inches off his seat, he collapsed back down. Then I saw him make a fist and pound the arm of the chair in frustration. I cried for him.[9]

Eva Silva, who had seen the pope in Denver, also attended the Toronto World Youth Day. "He's...old, and he's here," she told a CBS reporter at the scene. "He's ill, and he's here. For us! Waiting to see us! To talk to us! That's amazing."[10]

The pope did not want the youth to focus on his frailty but rather on their own abilities to serve God. "You are the salt of the earth.... You are the light of the world" (Matthew 5:13–14) was the theme in Toronto, and prayer was the means of becoming salt and light. The pope told the young people: "Look to Jesus, the living One, and repeat what the Apostles asked: 'Lord, teach us how to pray.' Prayer will be *the salt* that gives flavour to your lives, and leads you to him, humanity's *true light.*"[11]

## ABUNDANT FRUIT

"I knew I had a calling to the religious life, but... I was... afraid. I couldn't help but open up to that... in Denver," Sister Annuntiata Cornelio would admit nine years after she attended World Youth Day at the age of seventeen. Cornelio found that when she looked at the pope, she felt the air to be charged "with faith and hope." She said, "That zealousness was contagious. I felt I wanted to be a part of spreading the faith and really being a light for the world."

She found herself taking more pictures of the religious women standing behind the pope on the stage than she did of him. Dressed in their habits, they too seemed to radiate holiness. "They were beautiful. That experience awakened my vocation.... [T]heir witness... touched me the most. They did not do anything: It was just their presence."[12]

Sister Annuntiata was not the only young person to heed a religious call as a result of World Youth Day. Dennis Garcia, a teacher from New Mexico, made his decision to enter the seminary after his experience in Denver. He credited the "courage and vivacity of the youth, together with John Paul II," for igniting the spark that allowed him to say yes to his vocation.[13]

The pope's presence also inspired conversions, and not just at World Youth Days. Carrie Walters was a student at

Franciscan University but not a Catholic when some friends invited her to a 1999 youth rally in St. Louis. "When the Holy Father entered the arena, I was surprised and impressed by the feeling of being in an incredible spiritual presence. When the pope spoke, it felt like every word he said was directed right at me. It was exactly what I needed to hear at that time in my life."

The rally left Carrie with a lot to think about. "My perspective of the pope and the Catholic Church changed that day. I hadn't really considered becoming Catholic before then.... I joined the Catholic Church in April 2001."[14]

## ❋ 9 ❋

*Pilgrim of Peace*

In 1999 MANY PEOPLE IN THE UNITED STATES AND EUROPE feared what the year 2000—or "Y2K," as it was popularly known—would bring. Some believed that the world would end at the stroke of midnight; others that technology would go haywire because of computers that were not properly prepared to register dates beyond the year 1999.

For the Roman Catholic Church, the year 2000 was instead a year to celebrate with joy as it marked "the two-thousandth anniversary of the birth of Christ, her Spouse." Pope John Paul II pronounced it "a Jubilee Year, / a year acceptable to the Lord, / a year of mercy and grace, / a year of reconciliation and forgiveness, / of salvation and peace."[1]

The Catholic Church borrowed its practice of the jubilee year from the book of Leviticus and Jewish tradition. During this year of grace, debts would be forgiven, and slaves and prisoners set free. Originally celebrated every fifty years, the Church eventually observed jubilees every thirty-three years, the number of years Jesus lived on Earth. Over the centuries jubilees came to be celebrated less often and only at the initiative of the pope. The faithful are called to observe jubilees with special practices, such as going to confession and renouncing sin, making pilgrimages to holy sites, praying for the pope and receiving Communion more frequently.

Because the year 2000 was the beginning not only of a new century but also of a new millennium, and because it marked a particularly important milestone in the Christian calendar, Pope John Paul II declared it a *Great* Jubilee Year. He also decided that a three-year preparation period was needed to lead up to the celebration. This was best observed, the Holy Father said, through meditation, and he asked that people dedicate 1997 to meditating on Jesus, 1998 to meditating on the Holy Spirit and 1999 to meditating on God the Father.

There are four basilicas in Rome, each with a specially sealed "holy door" that is opened only for jubilee celebrations. The main holy door is located at St. Peter's Basilica. On Christmas Eve, by Vatican tradition, the pope begins the jubilee year by striking the wall (or whatever is sealing the door closed) with a hammer made of precious metals, as he utters the proclamation, "This is the gate of the Lord." These words refer to the gate mentioned in Psalm 118:20, as well as to the passage in the Gospel of John where Jesus describes himself as the gate through which sheep will find pasture (John 10:9), and again to Revelation 3:20, where Jesus is described as standing at the door and knocking.

Because confession is one way to prepare for a jubilee year, the pope bravely stepped forward and asked God for forgiveness for the sins of the Church. Although he did this in September 1999, he wore the purple vestments of the penitential season of Lent. He held a prayer service during which he asked for pardon for sins in seven categories: sins in general; sins made in the service of truth (that is, forcing the faith on others); sins against Christian unity (such as sins against Orthodox and Protestant peoples); sins against the Jews; sins that disrespect love, peace and cultures; sins against the dignity of women, who were "all too often humiliated and marginalised" and minorities; and finally sins that failed to respect and defend human rights.[2]

No pope before him had ever humbled the Catholic Church in such a way. What an offering to the Father! And what a fulfillment of Slowacki's prophecy about "a Slav Pope" who "will sweep out the churches and make them clean within."[3]

There was some opposition to the pope's unprecedented act of repentance, even among his own bishops. Some feared that in apologizing the pontiff would in some way "water down" the beliefs of the Church. But the pope never denied that the Church held the truth. He believed, however, that by definition the truth included forgiveness, humility and charity. Each time the Church acted against these virtues, then, it acted against the will of God and the Word of the Lord.

ELDER BROTHERS

From the moment he became pope, John Paul made an effort to continue the work he had begun as a bishop in building up relations between the Roman Catholic Church and the Jewish people. On his first visit to Poland as pope, he paid a visit to Auschwitz, perhaps the most notorious of the Nazi concentration camps, and stopped to pray at both the Polish and Jewish memorials there. In fact, onlookers expressed some surprise when he stopped first to pray at the Jewish rather than the Polish memorial.[4]

On another visit to Poland, in 1987, the pope met with Jewish leaders in Warsaw and made a public statement condemning the horror that was the Holocaust. He stated that through its suffering the Jewish nation had become "a loud warning voice for all humanity, for all nations, all the powers of this world, all systems and every person.... [The Jews] have become this saving warning... [and] in this sense [they] continue [their] particular vocation, showing [themselves] to be still the heirs of that election to which God is faithful."[5]

The pope showed his support of the Jewish people throughout his papacy. In 1994 he hosted a Holocaust Memorial Concert inside the Vatican. Sitting by his side throughout the evening was the rabbi of Rome, who had brought along his entire congregation; also in attendance were over two hundred Holocaust survivors.

Four years later the Holy See published *We Remember,* the official Catholic document on the Holocaust. The document took to task those Christians who stood by and did nothing while their Jewish neighbors suffered under Nazi oppression, saying that these Christians failed to live up to their calling as followers of Christ. It also instructed the Church to make an act of repentance for those failings and to work toward building a future of mutual respect between Catholics and Jews in a manner befitting those "who adore the one Creator and Lord and have a common father in faith, Abraham."[6] The Jews were, after all, the "dearly beloved...elder brothers" of the Catholic Church and were to be treated as such.[7]

Rabbi Abie Ingber of Cincinnati was grateful for all the pope was doing in reaching out to the Jewish community. He traveled to Rome with a Jewish delegation to meet with the pope on a Holocaust Remembrance Day in the 1990s. After installing a Holocaust-themed menorah at the Vatican, the delegation presented a mini-version to the pope.

When the rabbi had his turn to personally greet the Holy Father, he took the pope's hand and felt "an electricity that came from him to me and was reciprocated back to him. I never forgot that bolt of energy." That moment, that day, that pope, are all special to the rabbi, who has also said, "It is not important that I met the pope but that I met this pope, who brought communities together—who brought Jews, Catholics, Christians together like no one had done before."[8]

## THE POWER OF FORGIVENESS

The year 2000 was also special because it was the year the pope made a historic trip to Jerusalem. Following the lead of Christ, he wanted to take on the sins of others and make reparation for them by offering up a penance on their behalf. He stopped at the Western Wall, which is all that is left of the retaining wall of the great second Jewish temple in Jerusalem. It is considered to be the holiest location of Judaism and is the destination of thousands of people from all over the world, who come to pray and who leave their written petitions there. As a Jew who lived in Galilee, Jesus visited that temple on a number of occasions, most notably for the Passover before his crucifixion, and may have touched that very wall.

When the pope touched the wall, he inserted in one of its cracks a piece of paper bearing this prayer:

> God of our fathers,
> You chose Abraham and his descendants
> to bring your Name to the Nations:
> we are deeply saddened
> by the behaviour of those
> who in the course of history
> have caused these children of yours to suffer,
> and asking your forgiveness
> we wish to commit ourselves
> to genuine brotherhood
> with the people of the Covenant.
>
> Jerusalem, 26, March 2000
>
> Signed: John Paul II[9]

The pope did this because a pivotal responsibility of the Church is "[t]o evoke conversion and penance in man's heart and to offer him the gift of reconciliation."[10]

It was a real act of humility on the part of the leader of the Roman Catholic Church, one that has showed all of his followers—and everyone in the world, actually—that when we have done something wrong, it is best to come forward and confess it, for, "the essential act of penance, on the part of the penitent, is contrition, a clear and decisive rejection of the sin committed, together with a resolution not to commit it again, out of the love which one has for God."[11]

## FREEDOM OF FAITH

Extending love and respect to people of all faiths was of great concern to Karol Wojtyla, even before he was pope. At Vatican II he contributed significantly to the document *Nostra Aetate* ("In Our Time"), which states the official stance of the Church in its relations with non-Christian religions. The fourth section addresses Judaism in particular, and it states that the crucifixion of Jesus cannot be blamed on the Jews as a people. This historic statement made anti-Semitism an act of disobedience against the Roman Catholic Church.

Similarly, Wojtyla helped draft the Vatican II declaration on religious freedom, *Dignitatis Humanae.* Here he encountered opposition. Some Church leaders argued their concern that people might interpret the statement as saying that all religions are equally valid. Their fear stemmed from a misinterpretation of what the document aimed to teach. In actuality it did not call other faiths entirely true or equal to the Catholic faith but rather acknowledged that other religions had the *right to freely exist.* It also said that any use of force as a means of spreading the Christian faith is blatantly contrary to Christ's teaching.

## GLOBAL SCALE

As pope, John Paul could work on an even greater global scale and reach out to all peoples of all faiths. He did this in 1986 when he spearheaded the historic World Day of Prayer for Peace. He invited religious leaders from all over the world to meet with him in Assisi, Italy, to pray and fast for world peace.

As beautiful as this idea may sound, at first it was not well-received. Catholics worldwide feared heresy: Would the pope be praying with pagans? Fears of sending the message that all religions were equal stirred again.

The pope had prayed over the idea before even suggesting it, however, and continued to pray as he arranged the event. Eventually he put people's fears to rest. All the religious leaders would pray according to the dictates of their own faith, and the pope would do so, too. He was not going to pray to any but the one God, nor would he pray in any way contrary to or outside of the Roman Catholic tradition.

The religious leaders were assigned sites throughout the town, where they prayed with their own congregations for ninety minutes. Then they all processed to the grand podium that awaited them in front of the basilica of Saint Francis, where each offered a prayer. Then the pope made his closing remarks, and the leaders ended their fast by sharing a meal together.[12]

## EAST MEETS WEST

Pope John Paul II particularly wished to bring peace to the relationship between the Catholic Church and the Eastern Orthodox churches. The rift between these two segments of the Church had a long history. It started in the third century, when Emperor Constantine recognized Christianity as a legal religion and adopted it himself. In doing this he moved the capital of the Roman Empire from Rome to Constantinople. When he died his empire was divided between his two sons: one ruled the western region from Rome and the other ruled the eastern half from Constantinople. The two brothers and their respective domains expressed the Christian faith in different ways: Rome was more legalistic and heavier on doctrine, and Constantinople (Istanbul today) had a more philosophical and mystical way of looking at faith.

These differences came to a head in what is now known as the "Great Schism," when in 1054 Pope Leo IX excommunicated the patriarch of Constantinople who, in turn, condemned the pope. Thus the Church split into the Orthodox (or Eastern) Church and the Roman Catholic (or Western) Church.

The Bible tells of many divisions between brothers, and the split between these two Churches is not unlike one of those stories. The actual differences between them did not warrant centuries of separation, and John Paul II wanted to work toward healing the rift as much as he could. "It seems to me," he said, "that the question we must ask ourselves is not so much whether we can reestablish full communion, but rather whether we have the right to remain separated."[13]

The pope set to work on the issue almost from the moment that he became pope. In 1979 he traveled to Istanbul, Turkey, and visited the ecumenical patriarch of Constantinople, Dimitrios I. At the end of this meeting the two leaders issued a joint statement announcing the reestablishment of theological dialogue between the two Churches.

In 1980 the pope named Saints Cyril and Methodius copatrons of Europe with Saint Benedict. These two brothers of the ninth century served the patriarch of Constantinople in evangelizing Moravia; the bishop of Rome consecrated them bishops. The pope wrote an encyclical about Cyril and Methodius in 1985, *Slavorum Apostoli*. He kept working at improving relations between the two Churches, writing in his encyclical *Ut Unum Sint* ("That They May Be

One") in 1995, "The Catholic Church desires nothing less than full communion between East and West."[14]

The Eastern Church also made efforts to overcome the thousand years of tension and strife by welcoming John Paul to countries where the Orthodox faith is most practiced, such as Romania in 1999, Georgia and Ukraine in 2001 and Bulgaria in 2002. Despite his declining health, the pope knew it was important to make these trips. He told members of the Orthodox Church in Romania: "I have come...as a pilgrim to express the whole Catholic Church's affectionate closeness to you.... I have come to contemplate the Face of Christ etched in your Church; I have come to venerate this suffering Face, the pledge to you of new hope."[15]

## FAITH AND REASON

Reconciliation was also probably on his mind in 1998 when Pope John Paul II wrote *Fides et Ratio*, an encyclical on the importance of faith and reason and how without these two wings the soul of the Church could not fly. He quoted from Vatican I: "There can never be a true divergence between faith and reason, since the same God who reveals the mysteries and bestows the gift of faith has also placed in the human spirit the light of reason. This God could not deny himself, nor could the truth ever contradict the truth."[16]

Although stating that faith was the superior wing—perhaps like a dominant hand—he then appealed to scientists, to philosophers, to teachers of philosophers, to those responsible for priestly formation and to theologians to find the balance of these two wings in their pursuit of the truth. He also pointed out that a good means of fostering communication between believers and nonbelievers is philosophy. When authentically pursued, philosophy, he said, is a search for truth:

> Such a ground for understanding and dialogue is all the more vital nowadays, since the most pressing issues facing humanity—ecology, peace and the coexistence of different races and cultures, for instance—may possibly find a solution if there is a clear and honest collaboration between Christians and the followers of other religions and all those who, while not sharing a religious belief, have at heart the renewal of humanity.... A philosophy in which there shines even a glimmer of the truth of Christ, the one definitive answer to humanity's problems, will provide a potent underpinning for the true and planetary ethics which the world now needs.[17]

## SEPTEMBER 11, 2001

To Pope John Paul II, forgiveness and world peace were inseparable. And for someone who had lived through the horrors of World War II, forgiveness was the only answer.

The attacks on the United States on September 11, 2001, brought the threat of terrorism to world peace to the forefront of the world's consciousness. The following day was a Wednesday, and at his usual audience, Pope John Paul II expressed his "heartfelt sorrow" to "the President of the United States and to all American citizens." "Deeply disturbed" by the "unspeakable horror" of the attacks, John Paul said, "I add my voice to all the voices raised in these hours to express indignant condemnation." But then he added, "I strongly reiterate that the ways of violence will never lead to genuine solutions to humanity's problems."[18]

Less than two weeks later, while on a scheduled goodwill visit to Kazakhstan to meet with Eastern rite Catholics, the pope called for "Christians and the followers of other religions, to work together to build a world without violence, a world that loves life, and grows in justice and solidarity." He also said, "We must not let what has happened lead to a deepening of divisions. Religion must never be used as a reason for conflict.... From this place, I invite both Christians and Muslims to raise an intense prayer to the One, Almighty God whose children we all are, that the supreme good of peace may reign in the world."[19]

In November of that year, during Ramadan, a month-long Islamic period of penance, the pope encouraged Christians all over the world to join in the fasting, prayer and almsgiving of the Muslims.[20] He also called for another World Day of Prayer for Peace in Assisi.

### THE MYSTERIES OF LIGHT—2002

In the Roman Catholic tradition, one of the most powerful ways to pray for peace is the rosary. The Catholic laity adopted this prayer form centuries ago in order to imitate the monastic practice of daily recitation of the psalms. Many of these people were unable to read but were nonetheless eager for a disciplined and universal form of prayer in which they could take part.

The rosary's circular string of beads is broken up into five groups of ten beads each, known as "decades," with one lone bead marking the separation between each grouping. On each of the lone beads, an Our Father is prayed; a Hail Mary is prayed on each of the ten beads that follow; and the decade is completed with one Glory Be. Each decade calls people to meditate on a certain event in the life of Christ. These events are called "mysteries," and different mysteries are prayed on different days and at different times of the year.

Pope John Paul II found the rosary particularly dear because of its Marian emphasis. The bulk of the prayers recited on the beads are Hail Marys, and the name *rosary* means "crown of roses," an allusion to the Blessed Mother. However, there was one thing missing from the rosary, John Paul, thought, and it had to do with the mysteries.

Three sets of mysteries were used at the time, and prayed in rotation. The first, called the Joyful Mysteries, center on the infancy narratives of the Gospels—that is, the stories in the Bible that focus on the conception, birth and childhood of Jesus. The second group of mysteries are called the Sorrowful Mysteries, and they center on the arrest, torture, condemnation and death of Jesus. The Glorious Mysteries are meditations on the resurrection and ascension of Jesus, the birth of the Church and the reward of the Blessed Mother in heaven.

What was missing from these was a focus on the life and ministry of Christ. In 2002 Pope John Paul suggested a new set of mysteries that would do just that, and he called them the Luminous Mysteries.

Also known as the Mysteries of Light, the Luminous Mysteries focus on pivotal events in the life of Jesus:

1. His baptism, the starting point of his mission, when he is anointed by the Holy Spirit
2. His first miracle at the wedding in Cana, where changing water into wine prefigures his own death

3. The proclamation of the kingdom, by which Jesus teaches us how to live a truly Christian and holy life
4. His transfiguration on Mount Tabor, where he literally shines with divine light and is seen with both Moses and Elijah
5. His institution of the Eucharist, "the source and summit of the Christian life."

"Each of these mysteries," the pope said, "*is a revelation of the Kingdom now present in the very person of Jesus.*"[21] The mysteries feature five of the seven sacraments of the Catholic Church: baptism, penance, confirmation, matrimony and the Eucharist.

### THE YEAR OF THE EUCHARIST—2005

The Eucharist was also, in John Paul II's words, "a mystery of faith." And he declared the year 2005 to be the Year of the Eucharist, because "*[t]he Church draws her life from Christ in the Eucharist; by him she is fed and by him she is enlightened.*"[22]

One person who had been enlightened by the Eucharist was Marek Sotek, who at the age of four had decided that he hated the pope because his election preempted his favorite television programs in Poland. By the time he was in his twenties, however, Marek had grown to admire and even love the pope. And like the pontiff, he came to call Rome his home as he studied to become a priest.

On his way to the priesthood, Marek was ordained a transitional deacon in October of 2002. Soon afterward he was tapped to serve at a Mass the pope would attend. Flattered and nervous, Deacon Sotek suffered through a terrible rehearsal the night before. It was as though he had forgotten everything he had to do. And when the fateful day arrived, he was even more nervous. The Mass was to be televised, so any mistake he made would be broadcast around the world.

Just when he was sure he would implode from anxiety, he sensed a very strong and comforting feeling of peace emanating from one direction. When he turned that way, he saw that Pope John Paul II had arrived. Suddenly all of his fears were gone. And as he proceeded with the Mass, he was able to calmly remember everything he needed to do, completely convinced that all would be well—and it was.

Deacon Sotek would experience John Paul's deep love of the Eucharist in one final, special way while serving at another Mass in Rome. At that Mass he was given the privilege of bringing to the pope the paten—the gold-plated bowl that holds the consecrated Host—as the pope was mostly confined to a chair by then. When the young deacon deferentially handed the paten to him, the pontiff took the Host and ate it slowly, reverently. As Sotek thought to step away, the Holy Father gently placed his hands on top of his.

The young priest and the old pontiff were suddenly holding the paten together. Sotek froze in both awe and humility, and he remained there in silent prayer as his understanding of the "Communion" aspect of the ritual sacrifice deepened.[23]

The Eucharist reminds us that Jesus sacrificed himself out of love for all the people in the world. As age and Parkinson's disease continued their advance on the Holy Father during this Year of the Eucharist, John Paul's own participation in that offering would become clearer.

## ❧ 10 ❧

## *John Paul the Great*

MARCH 27, 2005, WAS EASTER SUNDAY, AND TO THE DELIGHT of the 110,000 people who had gathered at St. Peter's Square, the pope appeared at his apartment window to extend his traditional blessing. Having recently undergone throat surgery, he had not made a public appearance in nearly two weeks. It had been the first time in his twenty-six-year pontificate that he had not been able to preside over any of the special Masses that mark Holy Week, including the Easter Mass itself.

As the image of his face flashed onto the two jumbo television screens in the piazza, the crowd cheered and the pope extended his hand. He opened his mouth to begin, "In the name of the Father..." However, to the shock of the people below and despite the microphone propped in front of him, his strangled whisper could barely be heard. John Paul's hand flew to his throat, and his face contorted in pain, sadness and frustration. Finally he made the Sign of the Cross in a silent blessing and retired to his room. Many in the crowd began to weep.

By early 2005 the pope's health was deteriorating rapidly. He was subject to coughing fits and was quickly losing weight. He was also hospitalized and treated for a number of ailments, including a bout with the flu that resulted in his having to have a tracheotomy, which enabled him to breathe through a tube. Throat problems were to be expected: Once Parkinson's disease has advanced to a certain stage, muscular degeneration gradually makes clearing one's throat, eating, swallowing and eventually even breathing impossible. Now that he was no longer able to speak or walk, it was obvious to those around the pope—and to people around the world— that John Paul II did not have long to live.

After seeing the pope's Easter appearance, Father Marek Sotek decided it would be a matter of days. *If he doesn't die on a Saturday*, he thought, knowing that the Catholic Church dedicates all Saturdays to the Virgin Mother in a special way, *then it will be on Divine Mercy Sunday*. The Blessed Mother and the Divine Mercy were two of the pope's favorite devotions.

## THE MYSTERY OF SUFFERING

In his apostolic letter on human suffering, John Paul had written, "Human suffering evokes *compassion*; it also evokes *respect*, and in its own way it *intimidates*. For in suffering is contained the greatness of a specific mystery."[1] He had also noted, "People who suffer become similar to one another through the analogy of their situation, the trial of their destiny, or through their need for understanding and care, and perhaps above all through the persistent question of the meaning of suffering."[2]

In his last days he would live out his own words, since at the same time a battle was going on in the United States of America concerning who had the power of life and death over a young woman named Terri Schiavo.

Terri Schiavo was a forty-one-year-old woman who, sixteen years before, had collapsed in cardiorespiratory arrest. As a result she was severely brain damaged, and she had been placed on a ventilator. Although she was soon able to breathe on her own, she was unable to swallow and so was kept nourished and hydrated via a special feeding tube.

In the years that followed, Terri's husband, Michael, began asking doctors to euthanize his wife, arguing that her feeding tube was a means of artificial life support. Terri's parents, Robert and Mary Schindler, argued against him, saying that food and water are natural means that everyone needs to survive.

At first Florida law was on the Schindlers' side. However, by the spring of 1999, the law changed, redefining the use of a feeding tube as "medical treatment" or artificial life support, and the battle between Michael Schiavo and the Schindlers resumed. Terri's parents argued that their daughter's case was unique, since euthanasia was usually performed on the terminally ill, which Terri, although profoundly disabled and nonverbal, was not. If her feeding tube were removed, she would take as long to die as any healthy person would on being denied access to food or drink. Despite their pleas, the court ordered that Terri's food and water be cut off.

The world then watched and waited, as with each passing day Terri Schiavo was slowly starved and dehydrated. Meanwhile, the pope's health too continued to fade. News reporters compared the two cases and speculated on which public figure would die first. Terri did, on Thursday, March 30. It took her thirteen days to die of dehydration. Cardinal José Saraiva Martins, head of the Vatican office for the canonization of saints, was appalled upon hearing the news and called her death "an attack against God."[3]

That same day Cardinal Christoph Schönborn, the archbishop of Vienna, told an Austrian news agency that the pope was "approaching, as far as a person can tell, the end of his life."[4]

Supporters of Terri Schiavo's right to live expressed the hopeful idea that once the pope died, he might take Terri's soul to heaven with him.

## "WE HAVE COME"

"[T]he world of suffering...contains within itself a singular challenge to *communion and solidarity*."[5]

Throughout his papacy John Paul had championed the sanctity of human life, from conception to natural death. In the end he would be his own best example of what that meant. In fact, he was such a model of dignity in suffering that even his political opponents and detractors expressed their admiration during his last days.

Frances Kissling, then-president of Catholics for a Free Choice, admitted that she found the pope in "his ill health and his stamina in suffering to be inspirational."[6] Loni Ellis, a Washington, D.C., law firm employee who took issue with the pope's orthodox teachings on issues like contraception and homosexuality, said in a *Washington Post* interview that she could not help but praise him highly. She admitted thinking that the pope was "about as spiritually perfect as a mortal can be" and perhaps "the holiest man alive."[7]

The Reverend Charles E. Pope, of St. Thomas More parish in southeast Washington, understood the new waves of respect the pope was engendering. "Some people want to turn their face away when people are suffering, but for the Christian there is glory in suffering just as Jesus showed us.... And the pope is showing great patience in his suffering."[8]

On March 31 Joaquin Navarro-Valls, a spokesman for the Vatican, announced: "This morning, the Holy Father's health condition is very grave."[9]

While undergoing treatment for a urinary tract infection, the pope had suffered heart failure, and although he was conscious, the pontiff remained in very serious condition. Doctors from Gemelli Polyclinic had been called to his bedside, but the pope asked that he not be admitted there for care, desiring instead to remain in his apostolic palace apartment. Navarro-Valls added that the pope had been given the sacrament of the anointing of the sick.

Upon hearing this, pilgrims began streaming into St. Peter's Square. They wanted to keep watch and pray. Police set up a barrier to contain the quickly growing numbers and rerouted traffic from the main road that usually led to the square.

During the next two days the mood in the square became almost festive as young adults poured in. They tried to cheer their beloved Holy Father by chanting his name in Italian,

*Gio-van-ni Pau-lo! Gio-van-ni Pau-lo!* They also sang to the pope who so loved music.

Couples young and old, families, nuns and priests also showed up in droves to pray rosaries and lend the pope their support. Upon hearing how people had gathered to pray for him, John Paul whispered, "I have looked for you. Now you have come to me. And I thank you."[10] When this statement hit the news, even more young people flooded the square. A group of Italians came wearing bandanas of papal yellow and carrying a banner that read: "You called us and so we are here."[11]

Viviana Parti, a woman who lived near the Vatican, walked over with her father, Giuseppe. She noticed that even people who did not consider themselves to be particularly religious, like her father, felt drawn to gather and pray for Pope John Paul II. The Partis were literally neighbors of the pope, but it appeared that so was everyone else in the world. "Pope John Paul II," Viviana said, "shortened the distances between the Church as an institution and its public."[12]

Carlos Padula, a banker from New York, did not consider himself to be particularly religious either. On April 2 he was sitting on an airplane waiting to go home when he suddenly felt the urge to go to St. Peter's Square instead. Surprisingly, he was able to purchase an airplane ticket to the hottest destination in Europe at the moment and to get a cab once he arrived in Rome. His cab driver even knew a shortcut to the Vatican, one that could sneak him inside the piazza near the colonnades in the front of the basilica. And as a lonely Mr. Padula made his way through the square, unsure of what to do next, he heard some people call his name. It was a group of

Legionaries of Christ whom he had met a few years before. "Come pray with us," they invited.[13]

Also in the square was Sister Eva Hermana from Argentina. She remarked upon observing the scene, "There are many here, but across different languages, different countries and different cultures, we are all joined together in thinking of him. He has united us all...."[14]

It seemed as if all of Rome was praying for the pope. Father Andrzej Klimek, the Polish pastor of an Italian church in Latina, led his congregation in a litany of the saints, asking them to intercede on John Paul's behalf: "Saint Michael, pray for him. Saint Peter and Saint Paul, pray for him...."[15]

## "It Is Finished"

Meanwhile, in the pope's chambers, his fellow bishops also prayed. It was in fact a day of continuous prayer. Per his request, the Gospel of John was read aloud, and the bishops prayed all the prayers prescribed by the Liturgy of the Hours. The pope let it be known that he wished to attend Mass, so his loyal friend and secretary, Archbishop Stanislaw Dziwisz, offered up the Eucharist at his bedside and gave him viaticum, the last Holy Communion of a dying person.

Afterward, Dziwisz stayed by the pope's side, holding his hand as he struggled to breathe. The mood in the room was not one of sadness but of complete serenity and awe—and the prayers continued. Then, as the priests finished another set of prayers, the pope slowly turned his head to look out the window and, mustering the last of his strength, whispered, "Amen."[16]

Down in St. Peter's Square, many bishops had been leading a group rosary. As night descended, a hush fell over the crowd, and a familiar sense of peace descended upon Father Marek Sotek, who had been praying in the square for three days. Astonished, he looked up at his friend Father Dariusz Lewicki and asked, "Do you feel *that*?"

Father Lewicki nodded. "*He* is here!"[17]

Carlos Padula had been praying the rosary quietly with the Legionaries when he too felt the palpable peace. A movement caught the corner of his eye, and looking up, he saw a white dove take off from the ledge of the pope's apartment window and fly in a circle over the crowd. It was a brilliant white against the purple sky. When it returned to the ledge of the pope's apartment window, a light came on behind the glass panes.

Moments later Archbishop Leonardo Sandri, surrounded by cardinals, stepped out into the piazza and officially announced that Pope John Paul II had died. The time of death was 9:37 PM. The pope was eighty-four years old. After a few moments of silence the crowd slowly broke into respectful applause. It was finished.

Archbishop Sandri credited the thousands who had prayed for the pope with providing their shepherd with a pious death. Hours of uninterrupted prayer offered up from around the world had helped the Holy Father journey toward the Father in heaven.

And in the end, Father Marek noted, John Paul II died on *both* a Saturday *and* the Feast of Divine Mercy, as the vigil of a feast begins the evening before. It could not have been more perfect.

## ❧ II ❧

# In the House of His Father

IN HIS SIMPLE AND HUMBLE WILL, POPE JOHN PAUL II
wrote that while he did not know in advance the day or the
hour when he would die, he placed that moment "like all
other things, in the hands of the Mother of my Master: *Totus
Tuus.* In these same motherly hands I leave everything and
Everyone with whom my life and my vocation have brought
me into contact. In these Hands I above all leave the Church,
and also my Nation and all humankind."

The Mercy Pope who spread peace and forgiveness
throughout the world also added, "I thank everyone. I ask
forgiveness of everyone. I also ask for prayers, so that God's
Mercy may prove greater than my own weakness and unworthiness."

With a Carmelite sense of detachment, he admitted, "I
leave no possessions of which it will be necessary to dispose.

As for the things I use every day, I ask that they be distributed as seems appropriate. Let my personal notes be burned."

And finally, "With regard to my funeral, I repeat the instructions that were given by the Holy Father Paul VI [which refer to burial in the ground and not in a sarcophagus]. Let the College of Cardinals and my Fellow Citizens decide on the place."[1]

Understandably, many Poles wanted John Paul II to be buried in Kraków, since he had been archbishop there before his election as pope and he was perhaps Poland's greatest native son. However, even Lech Walesa had to admit, "A great pope should rest in the Vatican."[2] And that is was what the College of Cardinals decided.

Vatican II visionary Pope John XXIII had recently been beatified, and his body had been moved to an area underneath an altar in the main section of St. Peter's Basilica. Therefore it was decided that Pope John Paul II would be buried in John's former tomb. But first a funeral filled with centuries of tradition would take place.

Such a funeral demanded that Rome prepare itself as best it could for the record number of mourners who would pour into the city. Romans hurriedly stocked up on fresh water and set up thousands of extra beds. Officials rushed to line up additional trains for service. Posters of the late pontiff were put up throughout the city. The captions read, "Thank you. Rome weeps and salutes its Pope."[3]

LAST GOOD-BYES

The first official day of mourning was Monday, April 3, which began with the ritual transfer of the pope's body from the beautiful *Sala Clementina* (or Clementine Hall) to St. Peter's Basilica. There it would lie in repose until his funeral five days later.

The body of John Paul II was lovingly laid on a pallet covered in velvet, then slowly carried out of the apostolic palace by the Vatican's twelve official escorts, who wore white ties and white gloves. They processed first by the Noble Stairs; then through the First Loggia, the Hall of the Dukes and the Royal Hall; down the Royal Stairs; and finally through the Bronze Door and into the waiting crowd that filled St. Peter's Square. Spontaneous applause broke out as it had so many times before at the pope's appearance. For twenty-six years the Holy Father had waved his blessing from the back of his popemobile as it swept around the square. Now he was taking his last trip along that circuit, solemnly held high above the crowds.

As cardinals and monks processed along with the body, some people in the crowd cheered, others cried or crossed themselves, and many prayed. Swiss Guards stood watch in their final act of protection for the beloved pontiff, and just as at his ordination to the priesthood, a choir chanted a litany of the saints in Latin.

Wearing his papal robes and mitre, the body of the larger-than-life pope was now a small, nearly unrecognizable husk. His cheeks were sunken from the dramatic weight loss he had suffered in his final weeks. Decades of emotional trial and physical illness had left a frail remnant of the man who had once been so athletic and strong. But the crowd loved him still, swelling forward to be nearer to him as his pallet passed by.

Two million people filed past the body of Pope John Paul II in the five days that followed. Men, women and children from all over the world would stand in line for as long as fifteen hours. The basilica was open for twenty-one hours a day to allow as many people as possible their last glance.

Reporting sometimes at one or two o'clock in the morning, CNN correspondents Anderson Cooper and Christiane Amanpour were witnesses to the steadfast devotion. They each expressed feelings of privilege at being able to take part in not only a historic event but also one that witnessed humanity at its best.

More than once Cooper's eyes filled with tears. He couldn't explain the palpable aura of peace that seemed to hover over the crowd, but he could describe what he saw one evening:

> [T]eenagers sing songs about the pope.... [O]ld ladies clutch his picture to their chests....[4]
>
> It's so moving, even to be standing where we are and...hear this music and chanting just drifting across the air, sort of sweeping over Vatican City. It's a very moving evening...an extraordinary feeling...rich in tradition and ritual.... It's not just a sense of mourning here in St. Peter's Square, there is certainly that, there is sadness. But there's also joy, a celebration of the life of a remarkable man and an extraordinary pope.[5]

Amanpour agreed, noting that the crowd of about seventy thousand who were standing in line were "very reverent." She saw their sadness dissipate in the face of the desire to pay their last respects.

"You'd think that [with] these huge crowds there would be a lot of noise, a lot of hubbub," she said. "But, no, quite silent." Also notable was the lack of pushing, shoving and complaining, even though the line would move only in short bursts.

For some mourners the wait would prove to be too difficult. Despite their devotion and determination, they collapsed from exhaustion or dehydration. Others were buoyed to see—thanks to the enormous television screens that had been set up in the square for them—how quickly the line inside was moving. Once people made their way to the body, there was time only to make a quick Sign of the Cross and mouth a few private words of prayer before being urged on. Yet the flicker of opportunity seemed to satisfy the crowd.

"People are very happy to get in," Amanpour said.[6]

The mourning in Poland mirrored that in Rome, with sixty thousand worshipers turning out for Mass on the meadow of a church in Lagiewniki, outside of Kraków. Another hundred thousand came together in Warsaw. They filled the very square where Pope John Paul II had celebrated the Mass that marked the beginning of the collapse of the Communist regime.

## FUNERAL FOR A PEACEMAKER

The day of the burial arrived, and helicopters competed with the blustery winds that rushed over Vatican City and over the heads of the four million people gathered at St. Peter's Square for what was easily the most attended funeral in the history of the world. About two hundred world leaders, princes, kings, presidents and prime ministers were present, among them ten reigning monarchs, fifty-seven heads of state, three princes and the heads of the European Union, the United Nations and the Arab League. Charles, the Prince of Wales, postponed his wedding so that he could be in St. Peter's Square.

Flags of many countries, held up by people in the crowd flapped in the wind. Fluttering along with them were what appeared to be white bedsheets painted with black block letters that read "*SANTO SUBITO!*"—"Sainthood Now!"

When the simple cedar casket, inscribed with the papal insignia of a cross and the large letter M for the Virgin Mary, was brought into the square, the crowd rumbled with respectful applause.

Cardinal Joseph Ratzinger, at that time the head of the Congregation for the Faith and dean of the College of Cardinals, presided at the funeral Mass, which was as international as its attendees. English, Latin and Italian were the most spoken languages in the service, but also included were bits of German, Swahili, Polish, French, Portuguese and Spanish. A family from Wadowice brought up the offering of bread and wine, and they were followed by representatives of Kenya, Burkina Faso, Mexico, Korea, Italy, Jordan and France.

The legendary peacemaking spirit of John Paul II was alive and strong at the funeral. At the moment in the Mass when the congregation is invited to exchange a sign of peace with one another, "in the spirit of Christ who died and rose for us," the leaders of Iran, Syria and Israel turned to one another and shook hands. At the end of the service, the leaders of the Eastern Orthodox Churches were invited to come up to the altar and pray an elaborate traditional chant as they circled the pope's coffin.

Following Vatican tradition, the book of the Gospels was placed on top of the coffin at the beginning of the Mass to symbolize the Book of Life. It was left open in order to allow its pages to turn in the wind, symbolic of the chapters in the life of the pope and his effort to reflect the life of Christ. Interestingly, however, at some point during the Mass the book closed *completely,* as if to say, "This story has now ended."

The story of Karol Józef Wojtyla is the story of a man of faith who took on the sonship of Christ and served his Father with love. It is about a man who stood watch over the sacrifice of Christ in the Mass even as the world around him seemed to be exploding in every corner, knowing the world needed the offering of the Lord more than ever. Karol Wojtyla was a man whose first instinct after he had finished that sacrifice was to "go home" and see to his father's needs. He was a man whose call was to serve as the chief shepherd in the "Father's house" of the Vatican, a man who said on his deathbed, "Let me go to the house of the Father."[7]

"We can be sure that our beloved Pope is standing today at the window of the Father's house," Cardinal Ratzinger said as he ended his homily at the funeral, "that he sees us and blesses us. Yes, bless us, Holy Father. We entrust your dear soul to the Mother of God, your Mother, who guided you each day and who will guide you now to the eternal glory of her Son, our Lord Jesus Christ. Amen."[8]

# An Answered Prayer

A YOUNG ITALIAN WOMAN AND JOURNALIST JOINED THE thousands who stood in line to say their final good-byes when the pope's body rested in St. Peter's Basilica. Certain that Pope John Paul II had been a saint while on Earth and was now one in heaven, she had a special favor to ask of him. Her greatest desire was to be a mother, but she had been told by doctors that she had no hope of conceiving.

The woman was in a romantic relationship, she was not married, and she had fallen away from the Church. Standing before the body of the pope, she promised that she would return to regular worship and be married in the Church if John Paul II would intercede on her behalf for the gift of a child. If the Lord allowed this miracle to happen, she concluded, she would name the child after the pope.

Soon after she asked for the pope's intercession, the woman discovered that she was pregnant. She joyfully kept her promise and returned to her faith. She was married in the Church, then she gave birth to a healthy girl, whom she named Karola.

A few weeks after her daughter was born, she was walking down a Roman street, proudly pushing her baby in a stroller, when a dark car pulled up beside her. The driver called out to her, and the window of the passenger seat rolled down to reveal Pope Benedict XVI. He gestured for the woman to come over, and he asked to bless her child. After blessing and kissing baby Karola, Pope Benedict told his driver, "Now we can continue."[1]

The spirit of Pope John Paul II lives on.

# Some of the Writings of Pope John Paul II

The writing ability that Karol Wojtyla discovered and developed in his youth was evident throughout his years as priest, bishop, cardinal and pope. Following are some of his notable works.

## BOOKS

*Crossing the Threshold of Hope.* Knopf, 1995. Based on interviews with Italian journalists, the pope speaks about the existence of God, human dignity, pain and suffering and many other topics close to his heart.

*Gift and Mystery: On the Fiftieth Anniversary of My Priestly Ordination.* Image, 1999. An autobiographical account of the pope's journey to the priesthood.

*Love and Responsibility.* Farrar, Straus and Giroux, 1981. A defense of the Catholic view of marriage and sexuality.

*Memory and Identity: Conversations at the Dawn of a Millennium.* Rizzoli, 2005. Based on interviews with Polish philosophers, it includes a discussion of the problem of evil and the nature of freedom.

*The Poetry of Pope John Paul II: Roman Triptych Meditations.* USCCB, 2003. A short illustrated volume of poetry that John Paul wrote during his papacy.

*Rise, Let Us Be on Our Way.* Warner, 2004. An autobiographical account of the pope's years as a bishop.

*Sign of Contradiction.* Seabury, 1979. The first full-length book published after Karol Wojtyla became pope, based on a series of spiritual exercises he presented to Pope Paul VI, the papal household and the Roman curia.

*The Theology of the Body: Human Love in the Divine Plan.* Pauline, 1997. A presentation of the pope's weekly audiences from September 1979 to November 1984, in which he presented "a catechesis on the bodily dimension of human personhood, sexuality, and marriage in the light of biblical revelation" (foreword, p. 16). The appendix of this volume includes Pope Paul VI's *Humanae Vitae*, Pope John Paul II's letter *On the Dignity and Vocation of Women* and his encyclical *The Gospel of Life.*

*Theotokos—Woman, Mother, Disciple: A Catechesis on Mary, Mother of God.* Pauline, 1999. An easy-to-read collection of addresses the pope gave on Mary.

ENCYCLICALS

*Centesimus Annus,* "On the Hundredth Anniversary of *Rerum Novarum.*" May 1, 1991.

*Dives in Misericordia,* "The Mercy of God," November 30, 1980.

*Dominum et Vivificantem,* "Lord and Giver of Life: On the Holy Spirit in the Life of the Church and the World." May 18, 1986.

*Ecclesia De Eucharistia*, "The Church and the Eucharist." April 17, 2003.

*Evangelium Vitae*, "The Gospel of Life." March 25, 1995.

*Fides et Ratio*, "Faith and Reason." September 14, 1998.

*Laborem Exercens*, "On Human Work: On the Ninetieth Anniversary of *Rerum Novarum*." September 14, 1981.

*Redemptor Hominis*, "The Redeemer of Man." March 4, 1979.

*Redemptoris Mater*, "The Mother of the Redeemer." March 25, 1987.

*Redemptoris Missio*, "The Mission of Christ the Redeemer." December 7, 1990.

*Slavorum Apostoli*, "The Apostles of the Slavic Peoples." June 2, 1985.

*Sollicitudo Rei Socialis*, "The Social Concern of the Church." December 30, 1987.

*Ut Unum Sint*, "On Commitment to Ecumenism." May 25, 1995.

*Veritatis Splendor*, "The Splendor of Truth." August 6, 1993.

APOSTOLIC LETTERS
*Mane Nobiscum Domine*, "For the Year of the Eucharist." October 7, 2004.

*Misericordia Dei*, "On Certain Aspects of the Celebration of the Sacrament of Penance." May 2, 2002.

*Mulieris Dignitatem*. "On the Dignity and Vocation of Women." August 15, 1988.

*Novo Millennio Ineunte*, "At the Beginning of the New Millennium." January 6, 2001.

*Rosarium Virginis Mariae*, "The Most Holy Rosary of the Virgin Mary." October 16, 2002.

*Salvifici Doloris*, "On the Christian Meaning of Human Suffering." February 11, 1984.

*Spiritus et Sponsa*, "On the Fortieth Anniversary of the Constitution *Sacrosanctum Concilium* on the Sacred Liturgy." December 4, 2003.

*Tertio Millennio Adveniente*, "With the Coming of the Third Millennium." November 10, 1994.

# *Notes*

INTRODUCTION: *SANTO SUBITO!*

1. Adam Nichols, "Her miracle worker," *New York Daily News,* March 31, 2007.

2. Pope Benedict XVI, Homily of the Holy Mass on the Second Anniverary of the Death of the Servant of God, the Supreme Pontiff John Paul II, April 2, 2007, available at www.vatican.va.

CHAPTER ONE: THE GOOD SON

1. George Weigel, *Witness to Hope: The Biography of Pope John Paul II* (New York: HarperCollins, 1999), p. 46.

2. Tad Szulc, *Pope John Paul II: The Biography* (New York: Scribner, 1995), pp. 99–100.

3. Alison Behnke, *Pope John Paul II* (Minneapolis: Lerner, 2005), p. 11.

4. Mieczyslaw Maliński, *Pope John Paul II: The Life of Karol Wojtyla* (New York: Seabury, 1979), p. 276.

5. Maliński, p. 275.

6 . Szulc, p. 65.

7. Weigel, p. 28.

8. Maliński, p. 275.

9. Weigel, p. 31.

10. Pope John Paul II, *Gift and Mystery* (New York: Doubleday, 1996), p. 20.

11. Szulc, p. 67.

12. Szulc, p. 70.

13. Maliński, pp. 274–275.

14. Maliński, p. 272.

15. Maliński, p. 275.

16. Szulc, p. 73.
17. Szulc, p. 73.
18. *Gift and Mystery*, p. 17.
19. Maliński, p. 272.
20. *Gift and Mystery*, p. 7.
21. Szulc, p. 91.

CHAPTER TWO: CATHOLIC UNDERGROUND

1. Szulc, pp. 100–101.
2. Behnke, p. 29.
3. Weigel, p. 52.
4. Szulc, p. 109.
5. Szulc, p. 112.
6. Szulc, p. 118.
7. Karol Wojtyla, "Inspiration," in *Easter Vigil and Other Poems,* Jerzy Peterkiewicz, trans. (New York: Random House, 1979), p. 28.
8. "Inspiration," in *Easter Vigil and Other Poems,* p. 29.
9. Karol Wojtyla, "I. Material," in *Easter Vigil and Other Poems,* pp. 26–27.
10. Szulc, p. 117; Maliński, p. 29.
11. *Gift and Mystery,* p. 36.
12. *Gift and Mystery,* p. 35.
13. Szulc, p. 128.

CHAPTER THREE: THE CHURCH'S SERVANT

1. Maliński, p. 94.
2. Maliński, p. 92.
3. Maliński, pp. 137–138.
4. See, for example, John Paul II, *The Theology of the Body: Human Love in the Divine Plan* (Boston: Pauline, 1997). This book is a presentation of the pope's weekly audiences from September 1979 to November 1984, in which he presented "a catechesis on the bodily dimension of human personhood, sexuality, and marriage in the light of biblical revelation" (foreword, p. 16).
5. Szulc, p. 196.
6. Weigel, p. 150.
7. The editors, "Preparation for Total Consecration according to Saint Louis Marie de Montfort," www.2heartsnetwork.org.
8. Weigel, p. 151.

9. Pope John XXIII, Opening Message to the Second Vatican Council, Believe Religious Information Source, http://mb-soft.com/believe/txs/secondvc.htm.

10. Maliński, p.163.

11. Weigel, p. 155.

12. Maliński, p. 173.

13. Maliński, p. 195.

14. Maliński, pp. 196–197.

15. Szulc, p. 256.

16. Szulc, p. 256.

17. Weigel, p. 203.

18. Weigel, p. 194.

19. Weigel, pp. 216–217.

20. Toni Pagotto, *Pope John Paul II*, Andrew Tulloch, trans. (Boston: Pauline, 2002), p. 38.

21. Alessandro Mainardi, *The Life of Pope John Paul II...in Comics!* (New York: Papercutz, 2006), p. 76.

22. Szulc, p. 264.

CHAPTER FOUR: *HABEMUS PAPAM!*

1. Poem by Juliusz Slowacki, Dominican Nuns of Summit, New Jersey, 1980 trans., www.monialesop.blogspot.com.

2. Maliński, p. 116.

3. Szulc, p. 141.

4. Szulc, p. 240.

5. Maliński, pp. 256–257.

6. Weigel, p. 236.

7. Maliński, p. 263.

8. John L. Allen, *Conclave: The Politics, Personalities, and Process of the Next Papal Election* (New York: Image, 2002), p. 121.

9. Allen, p. 117.

10. Allen, p. 129.

11. "Exhilarating Roman Experiences of Prof. George Menachery," indianchristianity.com.

12. Weigel, 252.

13. Allen, pp. 116, 117.

14. Szulc, p. 282.

15. Weigel, pp. 255–256.

16. Weigel, p. 257.

17. Interview with the author, January 2007.

18. Allen, pp. 120–121.

19. John Elson, "Man of the Year John Paul II," *TIME*, December 26, 1994, Volume 144, No. 26, available at www.catholic.net.

20. Pope John Paul II, Homily at the Mass Beginning His Pastoral Ministry, copyright *L'Osservatore Romano,* available at www.catholicculture.org.

21. Quoted in Weigel, p. 271.

CHAPTER FIVE: A NEW KIND OF POPE

1. Weigel, p. 258.

2. Weigel, pp. 288–290.

3. Weigel, p. 301.

4. Weigel, p. 304.

5. Weigel, p. 306.

6. Peggy Noonan, "We Want God!" *Wall Street Journal,* April 7, 2005, available at opinionjournal.com.

7. Noonan.

8. Weigel, page 317.

9. Lorena Mongelli, "B'klyn Poles grieve," *New York Post,* April 4, 2005.

10. Waltraud Herbstrith, O.C.D., *Edith Stein: A Biography,* 2nd ed., Bernard Bonowitz, O.C.S.O., trans. (San Francisco: Ignatius, 1992), pp. 64–65.

11. "Teresa Benedicta of the Cross, Edith Stein (1891–1942)," www.vatican.va.

12. "Teresa Benedicta of the Cross," www.vatican.va.

13. Letter to Mother Petra Brüning, October 31, 1938, as quoted in "Teresa Benedicta of the Cross," www.vatican.va.

14. Herbstrith, pp. 168–169.

15. Herbstrith, p. 180.

16. "Edith Stein," www.americancatholic.org.

17. Faustina Kowalska, *Divine Mercy in My Soul: The Diary of the Servant of God Sister M. Faustina Kowalska,* Notebook 1, no. 49 (Stockbridge, Mass.: Marian, 1987), p. 24.

18. John Paul II, *Dives in Misericordia,* The Mercy of God, no. 14 (Boston: Pauline, 1980), p. 41.

19. John Thavis, "Hardly a Vatican prisoner: Late pope made secret outings, says aide," *Catholic News Service,* January 23, 2007.

CHAPTER SIX: "O MARY, MY MOTHER!"

1. Szulc, p. 358.
2. Pawel Zuchniewicz, *Miracles of John Paul II* (Toronto: Catholic Youth Studio–KSM, 2006), p. 130.
3. Zuchniewicz, p. 130.
4. Szulc, p. 361.
5. Zuchniewicz, p. 132.
6. Weigel, p. 413.
7. Weigel, pp. 413, 414.
8. Quoted in Weigel, p. 424.
9. Quoted in Weigel, p. 414.
10. Pope John Paul II and Cardinal Achille Silvestrini, *A Pilgrim Pope: Messages for the World* (New York: Gramercy, 2004), pp. 56–57.
11. Zuchniewicz, pp. 138–139.

CHAPTER SEVEN: PAPAL ENCOUNTERS

1. Tony Melendez, www.usaweekend.com.
2. Weigel, p. 346.
3. Pope John Paul II, *Evangelium Vitae,* The Gospel of Life, no. 5, www.vatican.va.
4. *Evangelium Vitae,* nos. 1, 2.
5. *Evangelium Vitae,* no. 4.
6. *Evangelium Vitae,* no. 12.
7. *Evangelium Vitae,* no. 12.
8. *Evangelium Vitae,* no. 4.
9. *Evangelium Vitae,* no. 4.
10. *Evangelium Vitae,* nos. 78, 79.
11. Robert Vitillo, "Reaching Out to Those With HIV/AIDS," in Mary Walsh, ed., *John Paul II: A Light for the World: Essays and Reflections on the Papacy of John Paul II* (Lanham, Md.: Sheed and Ward, 2003), p. 142.
12. Zuchniewicz, pp. 50–56.

CHAPTER EIGHT: FOREVER YOUNG

1. John Paul II, Address at the Papal Welcoming Ceremony at the Mile High Stadium of Denver, August 12, 1993, www.vatican.va.
2. "A Pope Who Thought Young: John Paul's Special Rapport With Teen-Agers," April 3, 2005, www.cbsnews.com.
3. Szulc, p. 422.

4. John Mallon, "The Pope and the Young: What's not to Love?" April 15, 2005, www.catholic.org.

5. Renato Gandia, "Denver deepened pilgrims' faith," *Western Catholic Reporter,* July 22, 2002, www.wcr.ab.ca.

6. Pope John Paul II, Homily for World Youth Day's Prayer Vigil, Luneta Park, Manila, Philippines, January 14, 1995, nos. 16–17, www.ewtn.com.

7. Weigel, p. 750.

8. Walsh, p. 34.

9. "Conversions, and Conversions of Heart," Franciscan University of Steubenville, www.franciscan.edu.

10. "A Pope Who Thought Young."

11. John Paul II, Evening Vigil With Young People, Seventeenth World Youth Day, Toronto, July 27, 2002, www.vatican.va.

12. Gandia.

13. Weigel, pp. 684–685.

14. "Conversions," www.franciscan.edu.

CHAPTER NINE: PILGRIM OF PEACE

1. Piero Marini, "The Opening of the Holy Door of the Great Jubilee of the Year 2000: Some Notes on the Rite," December 1, 1999, www.vatican.va.

2. Rory Carroll, "Pope says sorry for sins of church," *The Guardian,* March 13, 2000.

3. Slowacki poem, as quoted in Maliński, p. 116.

4. Eugene Fisher, "Celebrating Common Heritage with the Jews," in Walsh, p. 190.

5. Pope John Paul II, Address to Jewish Leaders in Warsaw, June 14, 1987, www.adl.org.

6. Weigel, p. 825.

7. Commission for Religious Relations With the Jews, "We Remember: A Reflection on the Shoah," March 16, 1998, quoting John Paul II, Speech at the Synagogue of Rome, April 13, 1986, no. 4, www.vatican.va.

8. Cokie Roberts and Steven V. Roberts, "Touched by the Pope," *USA WEEKEND,* December 18, 2005.

9. Letter Placed by Pope John Paul II at the Western Wall, Israel Ministry of Foreign Affairs, www.mfa.gov.il.

10. Apostolic Exhortation Reconciliation and Penance, no. 23, www.vatican.va.

11. Reconciliation and Penance, no. 31.

12. Weigel, pp. 511–512.

13. Pope John Paul II, Istanbul, November 30, 1979, quoted in Ronald Roberson, "East and West, Healing the Rift," in Walsh, p. 200.

14. Pope John Paul II, *Ut unum sint:* On Commitment to Ecumenism, no. 61, May 25, 1995, www.vatican.va.

15. Quoted in Walsh, p. 201.

16. First Vatican Ecumenical Council, Dogmatic Constitution on the Catholic Faith, *Dei Filius,* IV: *DS* 3017, quoted in Pope John Paul II, *Fides et Ratio,* ("On the Relationship Between Faith and Reason"), no. 53, September 14, 1998, www.vatican.va.

17. *Fides et Ratio,* no. 104.

18. Pope John Paul II, General Audience, September 12, 2001, www.vatican.va.

19. Pope John Paul II, Post–9/11 Appeal for Peace in the World, Astana, Kazakhstan, September 23, 2001, quoted in "Vatican Council and Papal Statements on Islam," www.usccb.org.

20. John Borrelli, "Dialogue With World Religions," in Walsh, p. 196.

21. Pope John Paul II, *Rosarium Virginis Mariae,* ("On the Most Holy Rosary of the Virgin Mary"), October 16, 2002, no. 21, www.vatican.va.

22. John Paul II, *Ecclesia de Eucharistia,* ("The Eucharist in Its Relationship to the Church"), April 17, 2003, no. 6, www.vatican.va.

23. Interview with the author, February 2007.

CHAPTER TEN: JOHN PAUL THE GREAT

1. Pope John Paul II, *Salvifici Doloris,* ("On the Christian Meaning of Human Suffering"), no. 4, Vatican trans. (Boston: St. Paul, 1984).

2. *Salvifici Doloris,* no. 8.

3. Daniel Williams, "Ailing pontiff suffers setbacks," *Washington Post,* April 1, 2005, www.timesunion.com.

4. Williams.

5. *Salvifici Doloris,* no. 8.

6. David Cho and Bill Broadway, "Dignity Inspires Area's Faithful," *Washington Post,* April 1, 2005, www.washingtonpost.com.

7. Cho and Broadway.

8. Cho and Broadway.

9. Vatican Statements on Pope's Condition, April 1, 2005, www.cnn.com.

10. Stephanie Holmes, "Chants and prayers lift pilgrims' spirits," BBC News, April 2, 2005, news.bbc.co.uk.
11. Holmes.
12. Holmes.
13. Interview with the author, spring 2007.
14. Holmes.
15. Interview with the author, spring 2007.
16. Nicole Winfield, "John Paul II's last word: 'Amen,'" *Chicago Sun-Times,* April 4, 2005, www.BNET.com.
17. Interview with the author, winter 2007.

CHAPTER ELEVEN: IN THE HOUSE OF HIS FATHER
1. Testament of the Holy Father John Paul II, *Libreria Editrice Vaticana,* March 6, 1979, www.msnbc.msn.com.
2. Daniel Williams and Alan Cooperman, "Tens of Thousands Turn Out to View Body of John Paul," Washington Post Foreign Service, April 5, 2005, p. A16, www.washingtonpost.com.
3. Rafael Epstein and Philip Williams, "Millions expected for Pope's funeral," ABC (Australian Broadcasting Company) Online, April 4, 2005, www.abc.net.au.
4. Anderson Cooper, "On the Deathwatch," *Details,* June–July 2005, www.cnn.com.
5. *Anderson Cooper 360 Degrees,* transcript of "Pope Lies in State in St. Peter's Basilica," aired April 4, 2005, http://edition.cnn.com.
6. *Anderson Cooper 360 Degrees.*
7. The Associated Press, "Pope John Paul II's Last Words," September 18, 2005, www.CBSNews.com
8. Homily of His Eminence Cardinal Joseph Ratzinger, Funeral Mass of the Roman Pontiff John Paul II, St. Peter's Square, April 8, 2005, www.vatican.va.

EPILOGUE: AN ANSWERED PRAYER
1. As told to the author by an anonymous source.